THE OAKWOOD PRESS

Railways of the Baie de Somme

A Landscape with Trains

by
Philip Pacey
with
Roland Arzul & Guy Lenne

THE OAKWOOD PRESS

British Library Cataloguing in Publication Data
A Record for this book is available from the British Library
ISBN 0 85361 554 3

Typeset by Oakwood Graphics.
Repro by Ford Graphics, Ringwood, Hants.
Printed by Oakdale Printing Co. Ltd, Poole, Dorset.

Cayeux. In this view from the air, a few feet of sand can just be seen at the bottom of the bank of shingle, which is topped by the beach huts and plank walk.
Collection Philip Pacey

Title page: Pinguely 0-6-0T No. 101 and Buffaud-Robatel 0-6-2T No. 3714 waiting to depart from Noyelles in 1995. A drawing by Nicolas Novel-Catin, whose drawings and cartoons frequently embellish the pages of the CFBS bulletin, *Ch'tchot Train*.

Published by The Oakwood Press (Usk), P.O. Box 13, Usk, Mon., NP15 1YS.
E-mail: oakwood-press@dial.pipex.com
Website: www.oakwood-press.dial.pipex.com

Contents

A group of staff at St Valery station. Date not known.

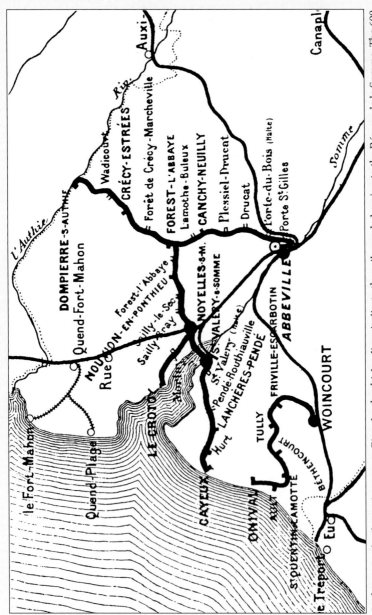

In this map of railways in western Picardy, the thicker lines indicate the railways belonging to the Réseau de la Somme. The 600 mm tramway serving Quand Plage and Fort-Mahon is also shown.

Introduction

I first visited St Valery with my family in the summer of 1992. I had somewhere, somehow acquired a copy of the excellent guide to the railway published by Les Editions du Cabri in 1988. Some of the colour photographs in this booklet, not least an aerial photograph of St Valery, together with the knowledge that St Valery could easily be reached by public transport, persuaded me that here was a perfect holiday destination. We were not disappointed. What I did not realise at the time was that St Valery had cast a spell on me; it would draw me back, again and again. Much of the enchantment had to do with the railway: not, however, with the railway by itself but rather, with the railway in space and time, in its geographical and historical context. I joined the Association du Chemin de Fer de la Baie de Somme (CFBS) and began to spend a few days each year staying in the small dormitory above the mess room at the depot at St Valery Canal and helping out as best I could, usually on tasks within the depot. After a couple of years I was very proud when my membership category was upgraded to 'membre actif'. But while sharing in this small way in the practical tasks which necessarily preoccupy the staff and active members of the CFBS, I began to investigate the history of the railway, driven by curiosity and by the extraordinary lack of a fuller acount, even in French, than that contained within the Editions du Cabri booklet. I became increasingly intrigued, almost to the point of obsession, by some unanswered questions and apparently yawning gaps in the received knowledge of the railway's past, not least with regard to the two World Wars. I also became friendly with two members of the CFBS, Roland Arzul and Guy Lenne, who share my interest in the railway's history, and who have helped me in my investigations and in the preparation of this volume.

Although this is the fullest account of the 'Réseau des Bains de Mer' (the two railway lines which comprise the present day Chemin de Fer de la Baie de Somme), in English or French, to have been published to date, it is not the definitive history of the railway; nor is it the book I would like to have written. The definitive history will surely be written in due course by a French author or authors, and I am encouraged by the fact that some members of the CFBS are now actively researching the railway's history. Some questions remain unanswered or only partially answered; more information will undoubtedly emerge. Unlike myself, French researchers will be able to tap unwritten sources. The present book is limited in its scope not least because my very restricted ability with the French language has set the parameters of my research - I can read French, up to a point, but conducting an interview in French is entirely beyond me. And that is why this is not the book I would like to have written. Had I possessed fluent French I would have talked to local people and former employees, and if possible to French people who had taken holidays in the area, about what they could remember of the railways of the Baie de Somme and what the railways meant to them. Sometimes, when I have been staying at the depot at St Valery, I have taken my breakfast cup of tea across the tracks and sat on an old turntable, gazing across the bay; or, after an evening meal and a *pichet* of red wine in one of St Valery's restaurants, I have lingered on my way back to the depot, enjoying the astonishing diversity of St Valery's domestic architecture, the quietness and sound of water falling through the lock gates, and (turning from the canal into the former station yard) the almost complete darkness which after nightfall descends on the depot and the bay beyond; at times like these I have felt intensely happy to be there, as if I belonged. But of course I am only a visitor, and a foreign visitor at that; in writing this book I have done the best I can. It is a beginning.

If my text does less justice to the human context of the railway than I would have liked it to, it does, to a degree (possibly more than the requirements of some railway enthusiasts), endeavour to see the railway in its environment. For me, railways and their surroundings have always been inseparable; there is much pleasure to be gained from looking at a train as part of a larger picture, and that pleasure can be enhanced by taking an interest in the pieces which make up that picture and understanding them for what they are and not merely as elements in a pictorial composition. The Chemin de Fer de la Baie de Somme is set in a remarkable landscape and, especially at St Valery, a delightful built environment (Le Crotoy and Cayeux both have much to offer, too, but I don't find them as enchanting as I do St Valery, and in neither case does the railway enter the town in such a way as to contribute significantly to the townscape). For those with eyes to see, there is very much here to enjoy.

I hope that for all its limitations this book will serve as a useful introduction to the railways of the Baie de Somme for English-speaking readers, that it will inform actual visitors and encourage prospective visitors. For me, writing it has been truly a labour of love, the next best thing to actually being there.

One small point should perhaps be noted here. The name 'St Valery' is sometimes spelt with an acute accent over the 'e'. I have taken advice and have been persuaded that this is incorrect (although it *is* correct for St Valéry en Caux, in Normandy). Certainly in archival sources the name is usually, if not invariably, spelt without an accent.

Departure from Noyelles: the train bound for Le Crotoy, hauled by Buffaud & Robatel 0-6-2T *Beton-Bazoches*, as seen from the cab of the train for St Valery, as both trains approach the place where the tracks diverge. *Ian Tate*

In preparing this book I have received help and support from a number of people. My wife, Gill, has tolerated, and even blessed, my annual trips to France; she joined me on my last visit prior to completing the book, in July 1999, when we were guests at the wedding of CFBS members Roland Arzul and Emmanuelle Moy. Roland Arzul and Guy Lenne have been invaluable collaborators, although I hold myself entirely responsible for any errors or misjudgements, and in particular for the inclusion of names of individuals in Chapter Eight. Even without his direct assistance, the book would hardly have been possible without the work of Guy Lenne as editor of the CFBS members' magazine *Ch'tchot Train;* Guy has fostered and continues to foster interest in the railway's history, not least by enthusiastically publishing relevant material in *Ch'tchot Train.* I was particularly grateful for his companionship during an immensely satisfying week which the two of us spent researching at Roubaix. Others whose help is gratefully acknowledged include Jean-Michel Candillon, Geoffrey Nickson, Maurice Testu and staff of the CFBS; Keith Clingan, French records officer of the Industrial Railway Society; Andy Hart of the SNCF Society; staff of the Bibliothèque Municipale and of the Département archives at Amiens, and the exceptionally patient and helpful staff of the Centre des Archives du Monde du Travail at Roubaix.

In addition to the individual photographers who are acknowledged in the captions to their photographs, I am indebted to BVA (Aloys Fauquez 93, 1018 Lausanne) for generously allowing me to reproduce so many of the historical photographs which they publish as sets of picture postcards, to the Ministry of Defence for waiving fees for the use of material 'deemed to be out of copyright', and to the CFBS for the use of photographs from their collection.

The CFBS can be contacted at B.P. 31, 80230 St-Valery-sur-Somme, tel. + 03 22 26 96 96, fax +03 22 26 95 96, e-mail: cfbs@neuronnexion.fr. The excellent CFBS Web site can be found at http://www.chemin-fer-baie-somme.asso.fr/

St Valery Ville station, built in 1937.   *Philip Pacey*

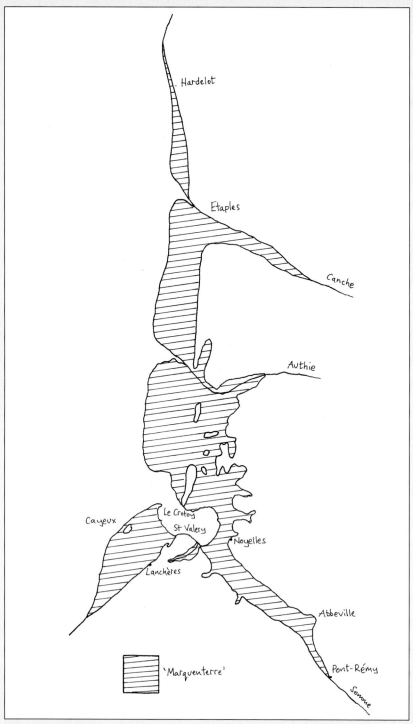

The coast of Picardy, showing the original coastline and islands, and the *Marquenterre*.

Chapter One

The Baie de Somme:
Landscape and People

Noyelles-sur-Mer is not actually 'on sea' at all; even in days gone by when tidal waters lapped at this tiny village's southern boundary, 'sur-Mer' was something of an overstatement, and the description has been even more far-fetched ever since the long, low wooden viaduct which carried the branch line to St Valery across the Somme estuary was replaced by a solid embankment. But go back further in time - 35,000 years, say - and Noyelles was truly *sur-Mer*, for the sea had not then caused itself to retreat by piling up *la plaine maritime picarde* (or *Marquenterre*) (*opposite*). This stretch of low lying land, from Ault in the south almost as far as Boulogne in the north, was created by erosion of the Normandy coast and the heaving of the resulting debris by the prevailing currents northwards, where it was deposited at the foot of cliffs which became *falaises mortes* - literally, 'dead cliffs', which the sea could no longer reach. Thus was made a new coastline, for the most part more suited to holidays than harbours. Before this, there was *no* Baie de Somme; today's tidal estuary was open sea, but for a promontory (St Valery) and some off-shore islands, including one which later provided higher, drier ground for the foundation of Cayeux, and a long one, running south to north from a point immediately to the west of what was one day to become Le Crotoy. The encroaching debris gradually blocked the mouths of rivers; the Somme, the Authie and the Canche insinuated a way through, in the case of the Somme scouring out the bay which, admitting the sea, gave Noyelles-sur-Mer its name.

The name lives on; the sea - which once sent tidal waters inland even beyond Abbeville to Pont-Remy - continues to retreat, and the bay to silt: natural processes accelerated by the hand of man. Human intervention is seen at its most dramatic in the form of the Somme canal and the railway embankment, but tracts of land have been drained, by means of canals and dykes, for agricultural purposes, at least from the 13th century. Since the second half of the 19th century, the most convincing *raison d'être* for the *sur-Mer* appendage has been that at Noyelles station travellers can change trains *for* the seaside, for Noyelles became the junction for the trains to the towns of St Valery and Le Crotoy, facing each other across the Bay, and to the resort of Cayeux, exposed to the open sea.

Although these small towns and the surrounding countryside share a long history of human habitation, nourished by the fruits of land and sea, they took on a new lease of life when seaside holidays became popular from around the middle of the 19th century. Previously regarded as barren and dull, the seaside came to be thought of as bracing and health-giving (not least in contrast to the grime of cities and industry), its popularity increasing as people ventured into the sea itself. Even before railways reached the area directly, people were using them to get as close to the sea as they could; after the opening of the line from Amiens to Abbeville in 1847, the Compagnie du Chemin de fer du Nord offered 50 per cent reductions on certain trains from Amiens to Abbeville on Sundays between mid-July and late September and encouraged passengers to take a boat trip from

Abbeville to St Valery. Leaving Amiens at 7.30 am, they could expect to get back at 8.10 pm. While the railways which were subsequently built around the Baie de Somme served existing agricultural and industrial activities, and provided year-round services for local people, they also carried large numbers of holiday-makers in season, acquiring a distinct (though unofficial) name of their own, the 'Réseau des Bains de Mer' - the 'sea bathers' railway'.

The Baie de Somme, as any bay, cannot be said to dominate the landscape; it is rather the sky which dominates, arching over the bay and the surrounding countryside. Yet the Bay, or the Bay and the coastline of which it is part, is the key geographical feature, around which everything else finds its place. A guidebook published in 1914 describes the scene:

> At Noyelles, the branch line to St Valery and Cayeux crosses the salt-marsh of the Somme estuary on an embankment . . . Ahead of us we see the immensity of the bay - at high tide, a vast lake flowing into the sea; at low tide, a plain of sand stretching from the hills of St Valery to the promontory of Le Crotoy, with Le Hourdel far away in the centre of the picture . . .[my translation]

The scene is little changed today; the salt marshes are visited by many different birds; by sheep; by fishermen; and by *les huttiers*, hunters who lie in wait in cunningly constructed hides covered in turf beside pools in which wildfowl may be tempted to land.

Amid the low-lying land- and sea-scape, the 'hills' of St Valery are the only higher ground. St Valery extends along the southern edge of the bay; above the main street a second, parallel street follows the contour of the steeply rising ground, so a higher layer of buildings, in a marvellous variety of styles, peeps over the roofs of those facing the quay which include a former salt warehouse built in 1736. The crown of the hill comprises delightful wooded meadows linked by a network of footpaths. This end of town is 'la Ferté' or the *ville basse*; to the west, the ancient *ville haute* occupies a fortified hill of its own - some of the walls, including several gatehouses, remain, and here are found the medieval church (largely rebuilt in the 15th century), the town hall, and the remains of an abbey. The town is named after a monk who founded a hermitage here in *c.* 610: his tomb is in the 'Chapelle des Marins' immediately to the west of the town. In 1066 the fleet of William - soon to be 'the Conqueror' - put in to St Valery *en route* to England, to await a favourable wind.

St Valery was for centuries a significant port; it remains popular with yachts and today accommodates a floating marina. In the last two weeks of July 1890, the port received ships bringing timber from Norway, china clay from Newcastle, soap from Nantes, coal from Mithil, and ballast from Hamburg; departing ships carried *silex* (whole or crushed flint pebbles or *galets*) to Weston Point, Newcastle and Norway, phosphates to Marennes, Tonnay-Charente, and Fleetwood, and ballast to Norway. The 1914 guidebook states that a regatta took place every August (10th-25th), and that the port could receive ships 'with a capacity of 5m - 5m 50', although the approach to St Valery 'presents some difficulties'. An English couple, Bill and Laurel Cooper, have more recently confirmed that 'St-Valery is an awkward port to enter', in their account of an inland voyage from St Valery to the Camargue, *Watersteps through France: '. . .* French high tides are higher, and low tides are lower, than those only a comparatively short distance away across the Channel', and for this reason boats queue up at the bar, then enter the bay together on the high tide in often spectacular *ad hoc* flotillas. The channel which enables boats to enter the Bay is constantly shifting, its course being marked by buoys, while the immediate approach to St Valery has from the 1970s been stabilised by means of an underwater dike marked by posts bearing lights. Cargo boats continued to visit the port, if less and less frequently, into the 1980s; a brothel serving the needs of sailors, located in an isolated house which still stands across the water from the present-day marina, remained in business long enough for an innocent member of the CFBS, in the Association's early days, to step inside what he thought was simply a café!

Nowadays fishing boats are heavily outnumbered by yachts; fishing, and enjoyment of sea food, is part of the life of the bay, catches include *sauterelles* (small grey shrimps) and many kinds of fish; various species of flat fish can be netted at low tide. Mussels (*moules*) are a speciality of local restaurants, while elvers (*civelles*) fetch such a high price that fishermen have been known to fight over them. Traditional fishing boats called *sauterelliers*, carvel-built with a huge foremast to carry the mainsail and a smaller mast at the stern for a tiny lug sail, were succeeded by motorised substitutes equipped with a distinctive winch at the stern for hauling funnel-shaped trawl nets.

Although the Somme was navigable to the inland port of Abbeville at high tide, heavily-laden ships increasingly went aground, or were unable to leave port, during the 18th century. A canal from St Valery to Abbeville was proposed in 1778 and was built intermittently between 1786 and 1827. A major feature was and is the sea lock at St Valery; some years after its construction, the lock gate opening into the sea was crossed by the railway on a swing bridge, while a lifting bridge was constructed to carry the road over the lock gate at the other end to the new railway station. Lock and canal could accommodate fair-sized coasters, but today the lock is a quiet backwater, as indeed it already was in the early 1890s (1891 and 1893) when its tranquillity persuaded the artist, Boudin, to set up his easel here. At least one of his paintings of the canal depicts the sea lock with the lifting bridge leading to the station; another canvas captures the view in the other direction, looking across to the quay and the entrance to the port. It is possible to imagine that an indistinct, darker shape among the impressionistic brush strokes could be a locomotive!

Though a small town, St Valery comprises several distinct communities - the families of fishermen and others who made a usually modest living from the sea inhabiting La Ferté; neighbourhoods of smallholdings and small farms on the inland fringes of the town; larger private houses around Le Romerel and La Haute Ville. The 19th century development of the town as a seaside resort added more features - the splendid tree-lined promenade known as 'la Digue', built on reclaimed land between La Ferté and La Haute Ville; hotels and villas in a variety of architectural styles; even a casino.

While he was a child, the family of Edgar Degas, the artist, regularly visited St Valery for holidays; three decades later his brother René rented a house at St Valery and in the late 1890s Degas made several trips to stay with his brother or with a local artist, Louis Braquaval. In the course of these visits he produced a

Above left: A poster published by the CF du Nord to attract holiday-makers to Cayeux. The bathing huts are sketched in (beneath the windmill on the right); the beach looks to be entirely of sand whereas in reality it was and is predominantly pebbles, with sand exposed only at low tide.

Above right: A poster published by the CF du Nord to attract holiday-makers to St Valery. Date not known.

remarkable group of more than 15 oil paintings and pastels, based on views in or close to La Haute Ville.

Degas and Boudin were just two of a number of artists and writers attracted to St Valery; indeed, even before their visits, St Valery had become a much-painted town. Paul Huet, Eugène Isabey, Thomas Shotter Boys and Richard Parkes Bonington painted the waterfront; Corot visited the area in 1853. The Australian artist John Peter Russell spent some time living in Picardy and painted his 'Paysage en Baie de Somme' in approximately 1887. Other distinguished visitors to St Valery included Victor Hugo and Anatole France; the latter included descriptions of St Valery, and of a funeral procession to Cayeux, in his novel *Pierre Nozière*, published in 1899; in this same book, through the persona of Pierre, he recalled writing in rooms on the Quai Blavet, with a view across the bay and a breeze wafting the smell of the saltmarshes and ruffling the papers on his desk.

Across the bay from St Valery, Le Crotoy is clearly visible (part of the view familiar to Anatole France); most eye-catching of all is the white water tower at the railway station which is actually some distance behind the town, though from this perspective it doesn't seem so. Le Crotoy too is an ancient town; the base of a tower the remains of the castle in which Joan of Arc is said to have been held captive. In 1346, during the Hundred Years War, English troops led by King Edward III, marching with little opposition from a landing on the Cotentin peninsula, almost to Paris, then northwards, with the intention of taking Calais, sought a suitable place to cross the Somme. They backed off from the well defended bridge at Pont-Remy, but with the aid of local knowledge obtained from someone they had taken prisoner, they forded the river at Blanquetaque. Then, the chronicler Jean le Bel tells us,

When all the waggons were across everyone rejoiced and wanted to lodge in a large town called Noyelles-sur-Mer. They discovered, however, that it belonged to the Comtesse d'Aumale, daughter of Robert d'Artois, so they respected the town and the surrounding land for love of the earl... On the next day the marshals went off to a fair-sized town called Le Crotoy, well stocked with wine and other treasure - for it is a seaport - and took it easily. After wasting the surrounding countryside they returned with considerable booty of large and small cattle to the main army, which was heading for Crécy.

where of course the King of the French gave battle. But that is another story.

Le Crotoy rivalled St Valery as a port until the construction of the canal; thereafter Le Crotoy found itself ignored by all but its own fishing boats. But in the mid-19th century it too began to flourish as a holiday resort and a retreat favoured by artists and writers. Jules Verne lived here from 1865 to 1870, and purchased a boat, the *Saint-Michel I* (it was followed by two others), which he sailed in and around and far beyond the Bay. While here he wrote *A Thousand Leagues under the Sea*, which was partly inspired by Verne's meeting at Le Tréport with Jacques-François Conseil who for years had dreamed of building a submarine, while the Baie de Somme was the original for the Baie de l'Union in *The Mysterious Island*. Among Seurat's late works were two fine studies of Le Crotoy dating from 1889; evidently the artist walked a short distance from the town in each direction along the coast, then turned around to compose a picture of buildings, boats, and bay. Another artist, Toulouse-Lautrec, stayed here for a while as a guest of his friend Maurice Joyant from 22nd June, 1899. Colette was a summer visitor in the years 1906-1909, recording her impressions in *Les Vrilles de la Vigne*. She writes of the strange customs of the region, where some fish from carts (*en voiture*) while others hunt from boats; she watches children playing on the beach - some 'roasting on the dry sand', others 'simmering in the warm pools' - close to their young mother, who is trying in vain to read a novel; she recalls waiting in a café with a group of fishermen until the rising tide lifts their boats - all of them leave except one, who on being asked why he is not going fishing replies that he is not a fishermen at all but is dressed up as one for the benefit of a photographer who produces picture postcards! 'Je suis "type local"!' And she paints pen pictures of the landscape:

> The sun [sets] peacefully beyond the Baie de Somme, a damp and flat desert where the sea, retreating, has left behind rectangular lakes, circular pools, and red canals in which its low rays are reflected . . . The sand is mauve, with a sparse covering of bluish grass, some oases of delicate bindweed torn by the wind, their flowers like umbrellas veined with pink . . .
> The sea has gone out so far that perhaps it will never come back. But I know it will, stealthily and treacherously. You don't think about it - you lie on the sand, play, sleep, gaze up at the sky, until suddenly a cold tongue, insinuating itself between your toes, makes you cry out, and there's the sea, everywhere, having covered eight kilometres of beach as quickly and silently as a snake. Without warning it has soaked the book, stained the white skirt, drowned the games of croquet and tennis. Five minutes, and it is lapping against the promenade with the 'flack-flack' of a dog contentedly wagging its tail. [my translation]

As a resort, Le Crotoy benefits from a vast sandy beach extending westwards - the only *south* facing beach in the whole of northern France! The flat, firm sands were the scene of notable events in the early history of aviation. In 1908 two brothers, Gaston and René Caudron, converted a barn at the family's farm at Romiotte (near Ponthoile) and started building aircraft. Needing more space, they transferred their activities to Le Crotoy and founded a flying school which prior to the outbreak of World War I became the Ecole d'Aviation Militaire and continued in existence until 1928. Unjustly overlooked by English-language books on early aviation, the Caudron brothers contributed significantly to the development of aeronautical design in this pioneering epoch.

Although in the context of this study Le Crotoy is seen as an integral part of the Baie de Somme, it was also promoted as the southernmost resort of the 'Opal Coast', comprising the coastline northwards as far as Bray-Dunes, beyond Calais. For instance, a leaflet issued in French and English editions by the 'Northern Railway of France' (the CF du Nord) in 1933 sought to draw the attention of the inhabitants of Paris, Brussels, and London to the fact that 'The Opal Coast is only 3 hours away', and characterised Le Crotoy, with its south-facing sands, as 'The Children's Paradise'.

The third of the three towns served by the 'Réseau des Bains de Mer', Cayeux, is altogether different; to reach Cayeux the railway leaves the bay behind, climbing through woodland behind St Valery before making a long, gradual, perfectly straight descent across a broad expanse of fields until level ground is reached at Lanchères. Between Lanchères and Cayeux is another landscape of fields, flat and open, beyond which, to the south, the chalk cliffs at Ault can be seen. The line of cliffs actually extends inland; it is represented by a ridge which follows the D463 road out of Ault and thence the D940 to Lanchères. The low ground between these *falaises mortes* and the present-day coast is the 'Bas-Champs', comprising marine deposits which became cut off and protected from the sea by a natural sea wall of flint pebbles, heaped up and prolonged by the constant action of the waves; a large area of the *Bas-Champs* is drained by a system of canals and dikes dating from the 17th century.

Instead of enjoying the shelter of the bay, Cayeux is battened down to the Channel coast, protected from the sea only by the huge bank of flint pebbles which extends from Ault, to the south, to the point of Le Hourdel at the entrance to the Somme estuary. The retreating tide leaves the pebble bank far behind, revealing a sandy beach on which the Caudron brothers and other aviators landed delicate flying machines in 1911 and 1912. Although the origins of Cayeux can be traced back to the 7th century, and while the town and surrounding area have been inhabited through the centuries by communities of farmers and fisherfolk, the Cayeux of today, along with the strikingly named village of Brighton to the north, is essentially a seaside resort; the growing resort, including hotels and villas, edged away from the old (13th century) church and closer and closer to the sea; in time the old church was neglected and a new church built (in 1897). However, during more or less the same period, from the 1840s, commercial exploitation of the vast natural resource represented by the flint pebbles (*galets*), heaped along the coast and buried under sand dunes, grew in importance to both the south and the north of Cayeux, offering another source of employment and income to local people. This dual nature of Cayeux, as a resort and as a centre for the *exploitation des galets*, has characterised the town ever since. It has been suggested that the *exploitation des galets* may, if pursued too far, undermine the natural sea wall which the *galets* provide.

While each of the three towns remains remarkably unspoiled by brashness or insensitive development, Cayeux today has the slightly seedy air of a resort which has been bypassed by the rich and famous, and by all but the least-demanding tourists; my guess is that as a holiday haunt it is primarily patronised by French people from not so very far off, people who can't afford or don't want frills or thrills but who are content to inhale the wind off the sea, to picnic in the sand-dunes or on the sandy beach which is revealed at low tide, to bathe, to be fascinated by the infinite variety of pebbles, and to enjoy Cayeux for what it is; families with small children; people who come back year after year. Out of season, their spirit continues to be represented by a seemingly endless row of identical bathing huts (estimated at around 800 in 1931), and a simple board walk, stretching as far as the eye can see along the top of the shingle bank. Today, for all three towns, tourism is more important than ever before; though the railway which once brought visitors does not do that any more, it nonetheless has a part to play in helping to attract them.

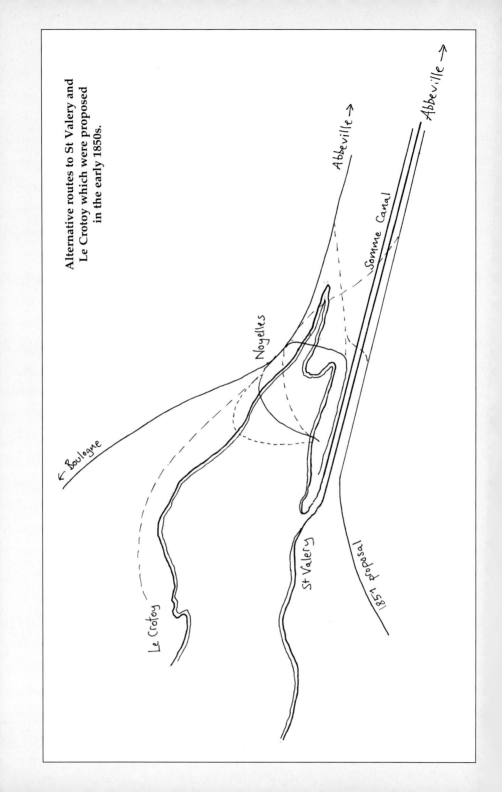

Alternative routes to St Valery and Le Crotoy which were proposed in the early 1850s.

Boulogne →

Le Crotoy

Noyelles

St Valery

Somme Canal

Abbeville →

Abbeville →

1851 proposal

Chapter Two

The Standard Gauge Branch Line to St Valery

The story of the 'Réseau des Bains de Mer' begins with the construction of a standard gauge railway by the Compagnie du Chemin de Fer du Nord from Noyelles, on the main line between Paris and the Channel Ports, to St Valery, including a lengthy embankment and a low wooden bridge 1,300 metres long across the end of the Somme bay.

Although a branch to St Valery from the proposed Amiens-Boulogne line had been envisaged as early as 1845, serious plans for such a railway date from 1851. On 17th May the Compagnie du Chemin de Fer d'Amiens à Boulogne proposed a second line from Abbeville, in effect running parallel with its existing route from Abbeville but taking the left (southern) bank of the Somme and following it to St Valery, then veering away towards Dieppe (*see opposite*). This proposal was submitted to a public enquiry advertised to take place on 19th June; it evidently did not gain approval. Only a few days later (on 9th July) it was agreed that the Compagnie du Chemin de Fer d'Amiens à Boulogne would be absorbed into the Compagnie de Chemin de Fer du Nord (CF du Nord). In a *convention* of 19th February, 1852, the Government granted the Compagnie de Chemin de Fer du Nord several *définitive* and *éventuelle* concessions to build and operate lines, including an *éventuelle* concession to build a single line from Noyelles to St Valery. This line was to become 'ligne No. 11' of the Réseau du Nord; in time it would come to be regarded as part of the company's *Ancien réseau* as distinct from the *Nouveau réseau*. But before the line was begun considerable discussion took place, first, as to the relative merits of building a line to Le Crotoy or to St Valery, and second, regarding alternative routes to St Valery and their environmental impact on the Bay. Le Crotoy was favoured by those who wished to avoid interference with the course of the Somme, and by the Conseil Municipal d'Abbeville; Abbeville, still an active port, no doubt regarded St Valery as a greater threat than Le Crotoy. Amiens on the other hand had no particular wish to see Abbeville prosper, and the Chambre de Commerce d'Amiens supported the St Valery option. In the end St Valery was chosen because as a port it offered greater potential for development. Several possible routes were mooted, but when it came to a final choice, two schemes remained. One, put forward by the Commission Nautique, proposed heading inland towards the Ferme de la Boullarderies, crossing the Bay at a point where it had narrowed to almost nothing, then turning back towards St Valery, the whole comprising some 10,000 metres. The other, proposed by the Compagnie du Chemin de Fer du Nord, envisaged a much more daring crossing of the Bay, reducing the distance to a mere 4,703 metres.

The Government ordered a public enquiry; posters advertising the 'Ouverture d'une Enquête' regarding a 'Projet d'un Embranchement entre Noyelles et Saint-Valery', and referring to the two proposed routes, were published by the Préfecture de la Somme on 27th December, 1852. The enquiry was to commence at the Hotel de la Sous-Préfecture at Abbeville on 24th

9. Le Pont du chemin de fer de Noyelles-s/Mer à St-Valéry-s/Somme (1,400 mètres).

F. Poidevin, phot.-édit., au Crotoy.

The *estacade* between Noyelles and St Valery. An undated picture postcard. Somehow the train is not very convincing, suggesting that it may have been drawn onto the plate by hand. The locomotive appears to have an open cab. Could this be an early postcard depicting a *standard gauge* train?   *Collection Philip Pacey*

Another view of the *estacade*. Undated picture postcard.   *Collection R. Arzul*

January, and was to last no longer than a month. There were fears that the changes which would be brought about by the CF du Nord scheme in particular would interfere with the flow of the tide and cause profound changes to the shape and profile of the estuary - erosion of sands here, silting there, which might variously have an impact on shipping, fishing, and hunting. The Ministère de la Marine called for a report from the Commissaire de la Marine; the Commissaire recognised that a railway would stimulate the area, including its shipping, and was persuaded that the lengthy bridge which was a feature of the Nord scheme would allow the tide to ebb and flow without serious hindrance. The Minister accordingly gave his assent on 26th October, 1853. Work began. The *décret impérial* issued on 17th October, 1854, confirmed that the Compagnie had to follow the route recommended by the Commission Mixte des Travaux publics in its advice of 24th October, 1853, that the building of a low wooden viaduct (*estacade*) 'destinée à conserver le jeu alternatif des marées' - designed to permit the ebb and flow of the tide - was a condition of the agreement, and that the construction work at St Valery must not obstruct shipping in the port or the canal. In fact, canal traffic was to suffer from competition with the railway from the day the railway opened, while the CF du Nord reclaimed and sold off land by means of a series of eight *renclôtures*, starting in 1856 and culminating in 1911-12 when the *estacade* was replaced by a solid embankment. These sales of land amassed a total of over 2,000,000 francs.

Detailed planning appears to have continued long after construction had begun. A 'Cahier des charges' (or schedule of conditions) of 3rd April, 1856, issued by the Direction des Ponts et Chausées, finalised details of the route only from Noyelles to 'piquet No. 30'. The CF du Nord was invited to submit detailed plans for the remainder of the route into St Valery. It did so towards the end of 1856, and its proposals for the last section of the route, including an extension onto the quay for *traction à chevaux* (horse-drawn traffic), crossing the canal on a lifting bridge, was approved, with conditions, on 29th January, 1857. Instead of a lifting bridge a swing bridge was insisted upon; a weight limit of 10 tons per wagon on the bridge was imposed. The company's initial designs for a swing bridge were subsequently rejected; modified designs were approved on 22nd June, 1859.

A passenger station was built just short of St Valery, at what was to later to be the St Valery Canal Halt and is now the depot of the CFBS; almost no signs of the original station remain, though the foundations of the main platform protrude through the gravel, and the gravelled approach, evidently laid out to allow vehicles to enter on one side and leave by the other, is an easily overlooked vestige of former grandeur. Leading directly to the station approach was a lifting bridge over the Somme canal of which there is also no trace remaining (*see next page*).

It seems that the station buildings were conceived and built as temporary structures (*provisoires*), employing a framework construction with brick infill, in the expectation that the station would eventually be relocated across the canal, closer to the town. The main station building comprised an entrance hall, a waiting room of 5 x 6 metres, a ticket office, and the station master's office.

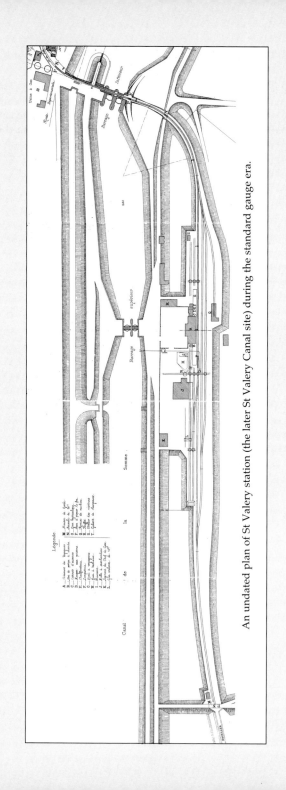

An undated plan of St Valery station (the later St Valery Canal site) during the standard gauge era.

There were in addition several other structures: a *cabinet d'aisance* (toilet block), a goods shed of 40 x 20 metres, an engine shed, a carriage shed, a cattle dock, and a shed for a fire engine. At Noyelles the branch line terminated alongside the main line station. Here too was a locomotive shed, a goods shed, and a cattle dock (*see next page*).

The normally hard-headed and entirely business-minded *Journal des Chemins de Fer* was unusually eloquent in its edition of Saturday 27th March, 1858: 'At St Valery, the embankments have finally been linked by the viaduct. This structure is magnificent; it wins admiration from passers-by walking between Noyelles and St Valery'.

At this stage rails had not been laid, but it was expected that the line would be open for the season. In the *Journal des Chemins de Fer* of 8th May, the CF du Nord mentions in its own report that work on the St Valery branch is effectively complete, and confirms that operations will begin at the start of the season. Thereafter, the actual commencement of operations appears to have been taken for granted; there is no mention in the *Journal*, and indeed I was beginning to wonder how such a significant event could have passed unrecorded when Guy Lenne and myself, working in the archives at Roubaix, came upon a reference, in a document concerning the provision of complementary omnibus services, to the fact that the opening of the branch had had to be postponed from the 1st to 5th June, 1858. (The *saison des bains* - the holiday season - stretched from 1st June to 15th October.) This then led us to the report of the opening which appeared in *Le Pilote de la Somme* on 8th June, 1858 [my translation]:

On Saturday the 5th of this month, at 4.00 in the morning, the first passenger train crossed the railway line across the Baie de Somme between Noyelles and Saint-Valery.

Descriptions of the station buildings follow - that at St Valery, though acknowledged to be only temporarily located beside the canal, is said to be bigger than the average station:

The interior is not finished, but already one can recognise that the arrangements and decoration of the waiting rooms are noteworthy. The shops and other buildings are as yet only represented by foundations just above ground level; the line beyond the station continues on the dike as far as the harbour, where wagons can be loaded from ships and brought to the station to form goods trains.

At Noyelles, work on developing the existing station to accommodate the new line was said to be still in progress. The reporter then described riding on the railway:

We took a train at low tide and returned on a train at high tide with the sea washing over the track; we can confirm that few railway journeys can be so pleasantly picturesque ['agréablement pittoresques']. Throughout the journey the traveller enjoys the most delightful view ['une vue des plus délicieuses']; at high tide one finds oneself literally in the middle of the bay, looking out to an immense horizon. It's like a painting by Gudin, a charming maritime scene: on the left Saint-Valery with its long quays, the silhouettes of which project to the edge of the water; the point of Hourdel, the sand banks and dunes resplendent at the point of Saint-Quentin while the movement of ships provides constant

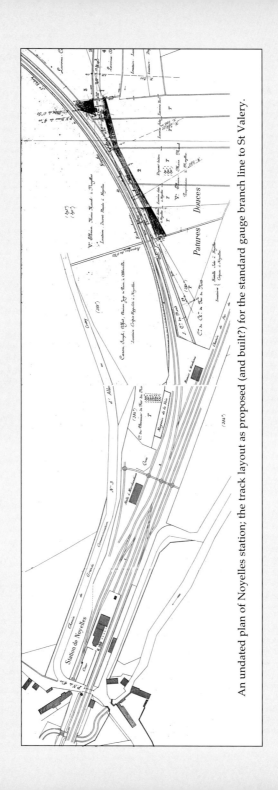

An undated plan of Noyelles station; the track layout as proposed (and built?) for the standard gauge branch line to St Valery.

variety. In the foreground are the verdant pastures which are already forming between the railway and Le Crotoy. One almost regrets that the locomotive hauls the train so quickly, because the journey is over in twelve minutes, and the train arrives in the station before one would wish to takes one's eyes away from this very interesting panorama.

No doubt worries about the strength of the long wooden viaduct had been aired; the reporter is reassuring:

The problem of the solidity of the *estacade* has been completely resolved. Movement on this bridge without equal is imperceptible; one is shaken less than on the ground; the train glides smoothly over the water like a sailing boat . . .

The report then describes local celebrations:

Although the inauguration was not marked by an official ceremony, the town of Saint-Valery was in a mood to celebrate. Every window was decked with flags, and so were the ships in the port. In the evening a fireworks display took place on the dike. Another surprise, thanks to M. Piéru [described as 'entrepreneur du chemin' - I take this to mean that he was the sub-contractor responsible for building the railway], was a huge bonfire consisting of a thousand kilogrammes of colcothar set alight in the middle of the bay. Its blazing light symbolised the triumph of man over the difficulties which Nature puts in the way of his great work.

Finally (having become more than a little carried away), *Le Pilote de Somme* concludes:

Trains already cross the Bay four times a day in each direction. At the station at Saint-Valery an omnibus service takes passengers to different parts of the town, to Cayeux, Eu and Le Tréport. The next step will be a railway to America.

Information concerning the operation of the standard gauge branch line between Noyelles and St Valery during the following 30 years is not plentiful. A train providing a shuttle service (*navette*) ran to and fro, giving connections to all of the main line services by day and night. The CF du Nord timetable, effective from 1st August, 1865, shows nine trains in each direction, with trains leaving Noyelles for St Valery at 7.45 am, 12.05, 1.45, 3.28, 4.28, 7.50, 9.00, 10. 15 pm and 3.15 in the early hours of the morning (meeting the 10.00 night train from Paris); trains left St Valery for Noyelles at 2.48 am (enabling passengers to arrive in Paris at 9.30), 7.15, 10.20 am, 1.05, 3.00, 4.03, 6.25, 8.20 and 9.43 pm. Of these the only train which does not make an obvious connection with a main line arrival or departure is the 9.00 evening departure from Noyelles, which returned as the 9.43 from St Valery, connecting with the last departure of the day from Noyelles to Amiens and Paris. The journey time between Noyelles and St Valery is in every case timed at 12 minutes. In addition to the regular schedule, even in its first weeks of operation, on 11th July, 1858, the branch received its first 'train de plaisir', providing people from Abbeville and beyond with the chance of visiting the seaside for a bargain fare; on this occasion a particular attraction was the regatta at St Valery.

A CF du Nord poster dating from 1858 announced fares for the new branch line. From St Valery, passenger fares were as follows:

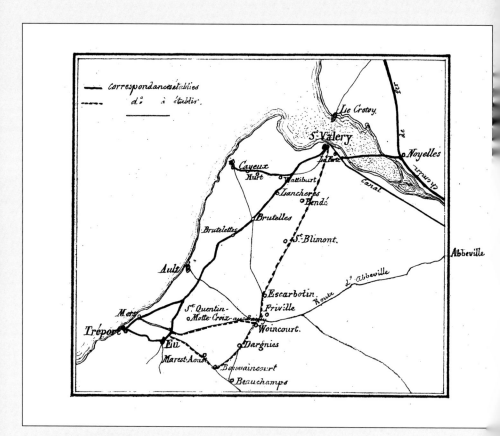

Omnibus routes connecting with the branch line at St Valery, 1858.

To:	1st	2nd	3rd
Noyelles	0.65	0.50	0.35
Abbeville	2.25	1.70	1.25
Amiens	7.15	5.40	3.95
Paris	23.75	17.80	13.05

Horse-drawn carriages (*voitures*) incorporating 2-4 wheels and a single inside seat could be conveyed on the railway at the rate of 56 centimes per km; two-seater carriages were charged 71 centimes. Up to two people could travel in the former and up to three in the latter for no extra charge. Hearses, with or without coffins, and including up to three living human beings, could be conveyed for 71 centimes per kilometre. A cow, bullock, or bull was charged at 22 centimes per km, a calf or pig at 8.96 centimes, and a sheep or goat at 4.48 centimes. A wagonload of animals cost 1.10 francs per km. In all these cases additional charges were levied for loading and unloading.

Motive power would obviously have been provided from the CF du Nord fleet of locomotives, but I have been unable to trace information as to which locomotive(s) worked the branch. A number of tank locomotives would have been available in 1858, including a series of 0-4-6 Engerth tank engines dating from 1855, and - surely the most likely candidates for operating shuttle services on a short rural branch line? - a series of 0-6-0 tank locos built by Gouin in 1854 and 1855. Weekly reports of accidents, breakdowns, and late arrivals, covering the entire network of the CF du Nord, located in the archives at Roubaix, offer some clues, and may yet provide answers, but I have only been able to sample these rather than making a comprehensive search. Thus for example, in February, 1859 there is a reference to locomotive No. 197 'de reserve à Noyelles'. Locomotive No. 197 was originally one of the 2-2-2 locomotives built by Alcard, Buddicom et Cie in 1847, which as virtually new locomotives worked the first services through Noyelles for the Compagnie Amiens à Boulogne (two locomotives of this class bore the names *St Valery* and *La Somme*). In 1859 it is likely that this locomotive would have been stationed at Noyelles for reserve duties on the main line. However, the CF du Nord rebuilt these locomotives into 2-2-4 tank locomotives in the 1860s, and it is conceivable that one or more of them spent their last years on the St Valery branch. Several, including 197, were scrapped in the 1870s. On 18th July, 1871, locomotive No. 432, on train No. 24, broke down at Noyelles - but was this a train on the main line? No. 432 was an 0-4-6 tank engine built by the CF du Nord itself at La Chapelle in 1857. Such a locomotive could conceivably have been working the branch line at this time.

On building its branch line to St Valery, the CF du Nord realised that it was nearer to Le Tréport than hitherto (58 km rather than 72 km), and so in addition to opening the railway, it also in 1858 inaugurated a horse-drawn omnibus service between St Valery and Le Tréport, connnecting with trains at St Valery. It partly operated the service itself, and partly franchised it to another operator, with extra services available in the summer season. A map (*opposite*) of actual and proposed omnibus routes appears to indicate that Cayeux was also served by omnibus, although no other evidence of this has been found. The proposed route via Woincourt and Dargnes shown on the map was under consideration following pleas from manufacturers in the area, notable for small scale, high

This kilometre post at the approach to St Valery Canal is one of several which survive from the days of the standard gauge branch line to St Valery. They indicate the distance *from Paris*.

Philip Pacey

quality metalsmithing, desperate to overcome their isolation and to benefit from the new communications. Nearly half a century later the same considerations would lead them to support proposals for a branch line to Ault and Onival, from the railway from Abbeville to Le Tréport which was opened in 1873.

* * * * * * *

While we can probably assume that this short branch line operated without fuss year in year out, yet there was a period of disturbance which affected the railway and life in general. The occasion was the short-lived Franco-Prussian War, declared by France on Prussia on 19th July, 1870, which virtually from the outset went disastrously wrong for France. Following the decisive Prussian victory at Sedan on 1st September and the capture and capitulation of Napoléon III, a provisional Republican Government sought to restore French pride. However, on the 18th September Paris found itself besieged, as Prussia took control of most of France north and east of Orleans except for Paris herself and some other pockets of resistance which, because of the strength of their defences, the Prussians opted to leave alone. Thus, trains - including the services of the CF du Nord on the line through Noyelles - were unable to approach or depart from Paris; railway workers and railway resources in Paris lent themselves to the service of a city under siege. The Baie de Somme, and particularly the port of St Valery, was of potential strategic interest to both sides as a means of provisioning troops. In October at Le Crotoy, the French requisitioned Jules Verne's boat, the *Saint-Michel I*, for the defence of the Bay; Jules Verne took command of a 'Dad's army' crew of veterans of the Crimea War.

French counter-offences, master-minded by Gambetta following his flight from Paris by balloon to Tours on 7th October, regained Orleans and held out some brief hope, although the loss of Metz on 27th October was a desperate blow. Belfort was besieged from 4th November, Verdun lost on 8th November. The Prussians now confounded French plans by interposing two Prussian armies between French forces and Paris; the Prussian 1st army marched towards the Somme, taking Amiens on 27th November, while the 2nd army blocked the route from the Loire. It was during the next passage of the war that the French 'Army of the North' under Faidherbe retook Ham, thus preventing the Prussians from using the railway line between Amiens and Rheims, and marched towards Amiens, which the Prussians had left in the hands of a relatively small garrison. When the Prussians responded by summoning larger forces under Manteuffel, Faidherbe chose to take up position some five miles north-east of Amiens. The ensuing battle, which commenced on 23rd December, was indecisive; the French army held its position but was not strong enough to take Amiens. On the night of Christmas Eve, the French retired to Arras.

The Prussians then took up position at Bapaume, threatening an isolated French stronghold at Péronne; Faidherbe moved to dislodge them and relieve Péronne, but his army was too weak to press home a slight advantage won in battle on 2nd January; the French abandoned their attack the next day, and Péronne fell five days later.

While the communities of the Baie de Somme remained on the margin of this activity, they were not unaffected. A telegram on the 30th December ordered the requisitioning of horses and equipment for the cavalry of the French 'Army of the North'; on the 31st, a consignment of saddles left St Valery (?) by the 6.00 pm train. On 1st January the main railway line was broken near Rue by a detachment of some 50 Prussian cavalry from a column *en route* between St Riquier and Crécy. This effectively brought the railway to a standstill, *including the metre gauge line to St Valery*. The CF du Nord recommenced operations between Abbeville and Boulogne (and one assumes between Noyelles and St Valery) on the 4th January. However, services to Paris would not be restored until May. The Prussians occupied St Valery with effect from 9th February; local communities subsequently struggled to meet the requirements of the occupying force for food for themselves and their horses. Meanwhile Paris, besieged and hungry, suffered bombardment, from 5th January, for 23 nights. Peace, when it came, cost France dearly; the price included Alsace and Lorraine, while much of north-eastern France, including the Somme, remained under Prussian control, pending the payment of indemnity, until September 1873.

* * * * * * *

Initially the CF du Nord had only sought, and been given, permission to use horses to haul wagons along the rails on the quay of the port of St Valery. Although this was part of the January 1857 agreement, more detailed proposals were submitted in August 1857 and approved in February 1858, and a further proposal to extend the double track on the quay to a turntable with a length of single track beyond was authorised by the Prefect in March 1863. It was not until 1885 that the company obtained permission to use steam locomotives on the quay; it appears that the Prefect could only authorise this with endorsement from the Ministry of Public Works, who insisted that locomotives and wagons should only be moved at night if absolutely necessary, and then only with permission from the officers of the Port and on condition that the trains were suitably lit ('à la condition d'être éclairés'); for its part the company undertook to ensure that locomotives moving at night would carry lanterns at front and rear.

The summer 1880 timetable shows 10 services daily in each direction. A very early departure from St Valery at 3.30 am appears to serve no purpose (there is no connection for Paris) other than to meet the night train *from* Paris; having done so, it returned from Noyelles at 3.58 am, arriving at St Valery at 4.10. Subsequent departures from St Valery were scheduled for 7.15, 10.23, 11.43 am, 2.20, 3.08, 5.44, 7.05, 8.50 and 9.55 pm, returning from Noyelles at 8.06, 11.10 am, 12.10, 2.43, 4.20, 6.15, 7.35, 9.18, and 10.26 pm. As was the case 15 years earlier, the journey was timed at 12 minutes. Travellers to Paris leaving St Valery on the 7.15 am could expect to arrive at Paris at 1.40 pm. Those choosing to travel overnight could catch the 9.55 pm from St Valery and arrive at Paris at 3.55 in the morning.

Chapter Three

The 'Réseau des Bains de Mer' from its beginnings to 1914

The standard gauge branch line to St Valery in the most literal sense prepared the ground for the metre gauge railway which was to come. In France as a whole, standard gauge was too costly a means of extending transportation beyond the network of main lines into rural areas. The 'Loi Migneret' of 12th July, 1865, had differentiated between lines of *intérêt général*, of sufficient importance to receive state support, and lines of *intérêt local*, which were to be the responsibility of the Départements; concessions could be granted to private companies to build and operate lines at their own risk or for an agreed recompense. However, at this stage narrow gauge was not invariably favoured as an alternative to standard gauge for passenger carrying railways, and the costs of construction of standard gauge lines, as well as the considerable formalities involved, continued to inhibit the development of railways in France.

On 11th June, 1876, the Prefect of the Département of the Somme issued a circular inviting the municipal councils to express their views on the possibility of establishing a railway network. In July the Conseil d'Arrondissement d'Abbeville responded in favour of the principle of building narrow gauge lines, so long as the local councils would not be obliged to suffer additional financial burdens as a result. The Conseil put forward several proposals, including a line from Le Crotoy, through Rue, to Noyelles and thence to Nouvion, Crécy, and Conteville, and a line between St Valery and Woincourt (on the standard gauge railway between Abbeville and Le Tréport which had opened in 1873) with an extension from St Valery to Cayeux (*see page 30*). These lines were not built, apparently on the advice of Monsieur l'Ingénieur en Chef who took up his post (a new post?) in the Département in August of the same year.

Another Act, passed on 11th June, 1880, sought in a number of ways to give impetus to the construction of light railways in rural areas. In addition to lines of 'intérêt local', a third category, of tramways running mainly along the verges of roads owned by the Départements, was designated; three gauges received official blessing - standard, metre, and 750 mm; and a scheme was initiated to attract private capital for the construction of lines which might prove unremunerative. By this scheme, concessionaries were expected to provide their own capital and to build the railway at an agreed cost, while the Département and the state undertook to pay a fixed rate of interest on the capital. The concessionary then operated the line and received a fixed sum of money per annum plus a proportion of the gross receipts. If receipts fell below a set figure, the concessionary was guaranteed compensation; this guarantee was met partly by the state but principally by Départements. Within a few years the scheme had to be dropped; as W.J.K. Davies has explained:

. . . this system led to a great deal of trouble for, since the operating company was guaranteed a certain minimum receipt, it had no incentive to develop the traffic. Indeed, it was in the company's interest to discourage extra work since this only raised its

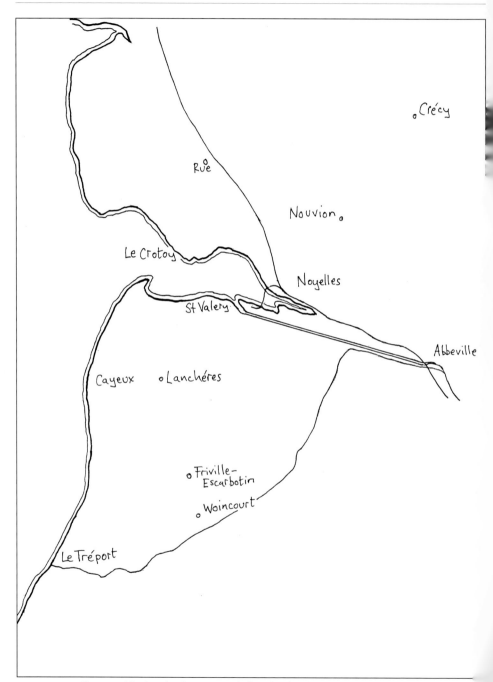

Communities involved in proposals for a local railway network, 1876-1883.

working expenses! And since, with no previous experience of such ventures to draw on, the initial estimates for construction costs and minimum guaranteed earnings were fixed at far too high a figure, the position was very unsatisfactory for all but the concessionary companies involved. [*Light railways* p.84]

In place of this scheme, Départements *either* built and equipped lines themselves and then leased an operating concession to a concessionary, or subsidised an independent company to build and run a line on terms which encouraged efficient working. These concessions were (and in some instances still are) relatively short term arrangements, often of 15 years, providing Départements with opportunities to invite bids from other companies or even to take over the running of lines themselves. However, before the earlier scheme was abandoned a number of companies obtained long-term 'concessions', and a few of them amassed considerable empires. One of these was the Société Générale des Chemins de Fer Economiques (SE). It was the SE which in 1884 obtained the 99-year concession for the metre gauge 'Réseau de la Somme'. These arrangements explain why Départements (and their executive heads, the Prefects), remained, and indeed remain, so directly involved in the running of the railways; the infrastructure of the Baie de Somme railway is to this day owned by the Département de la Somme which, in 1998, confirmed the CFBS as responsible for running the railway for a further period of 10 years.

Scarcely had the new Act been passed when, on 12th August, 1880, the Conseil d'Arrondissement d'Abbeville put forward fresh proposals, including a proposal for a narrow gauge line from Le Crotoy to Rue, and, again, a projected line from Woincourt via Friville Escarbotin to St Valery, with a branch from a point at or near Lanchères to Cayeux. On 17th August, 1880, the Conseil d'Arrondissement d'Abbeville expressed a desire that a line to Le Crotoy should also serve Rue. On 22nd August the Conseil Municipal de Cayeux expressed their desire for a railway between Cayeux and St Valery. On 30th August the Conseil Général of the Département received a report commenting on the differing proposals, and recommending a homogeneous network built to metre gauge at an estimated cost of 60-70,000 francs per kilometre. Lines to be built as a first priority included Woincourt to St Valery, with a possible branch to Cayeux but nothing else in the immediate environs of the Somme estuary; a group of proposals given second priority included Le Crotoy to Crécy via Noyelles and Nouvion.

No progress having been made 12 months later, two Le Crotoy residents, including the Mayor, together with a M. Guerlain from Paris and a M. De Savoye of Noyelles, all four members of a committee formed to bring about the establishment of a narrow gauge railway from Noyelles to Le Crotoy, proposed to the Conseil Général a line of 750 mm gauge, built on existing dikes to save money, approaching Noyelles between the main line and the line between Noyelles for St Valery, in order to avoid crossing the latter on a bridge. A pilot study followed, dated 21st September. The following month a pilot study for a line from St Valery to Cayeux was completed (21st October) and submitted to a public enquiry (which opened on 27th October). A document dated 30th March, 1882, refers to projects for 750 mm gauge lines between Noyelles and Le Crotoy and St Valery and Cayeux. On 6th October, 1882, the *Journal Officiel* reported

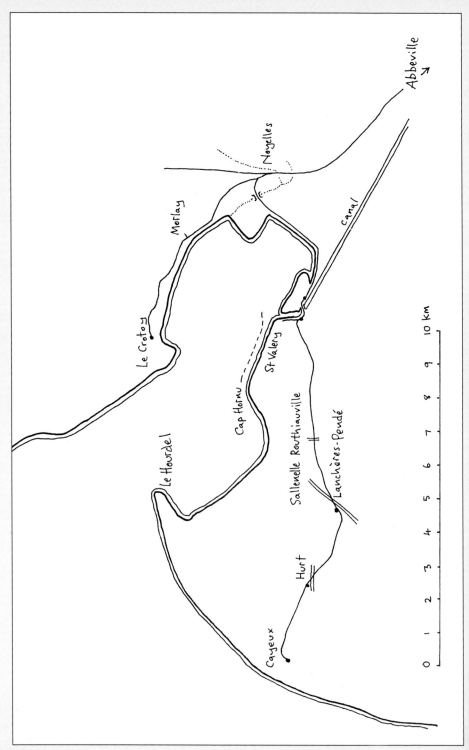

The 'Réseau des Bains de Mer', opened in 1887.

new calculations for a railway network for the Somme department, comprising some 300 Km of railway, of which 197 kms were to be built within three years at a cost of 60,000 francs per km (metre gauge) or 48,000 francs per km (750 mm gauge). On 17th March, 1883, the Conseil Municipal of Rue expressed opposition to the projected line from Noyelles to Le Crotoy (which would by-pass Rue).

Many proposals, many plans, no little anxiety from towns and villages which stood to benefit from a rail link, or to be disadvantaged by being passed by. But would anything actually be done? And, although the notion of a Département-wide network of lines of *intérêt local* had been articulated, within this wider context it had only recently begun to be envisaged that railways serving the north and south sides of the Baie de Somme might connect with each other. It was the SE's role as concessionaire, established in 1884, which was to facilitate the creation of the Réseau de Somme; and it was this and a deal struck between the SE and the CF du Nord, which was to be decisive in bringing into being the future 'Réseau des Bains de Mer'.

The metre gauge line from Noyelles to the fishing village and seaside resort of Le Crotoy, on the northern side of the Baie de Somme, was opened on 1st July, 1887. *Le Pilote de la Somme* of 1st July carried the following report:

Yesterday the official opening of the railway line from Noyelles to Le Crotoy took place . . . At 11.40 a special train left Amiens for Noyelles bringing the Prefect of the Somme, the 'Conseiller Général du canton de Nouvion', members of the 'commission de réception' of the line, M. Levet, director of the Société des chemins de fer économiques, and engineers of the Société and of the 'Compagnie du Nord'. When the train arrived at Noyelles, the mayor of Noyelles welcomed the visitors. [Representatives of] the town of Le Crotoy also welcomed the visitors, who returned to Amiens on a special train at 3.05. Now that the opening of this new line has been officially confirmed, four trains will leave for Le Crotoy every day, connecting with morning and afternoon trains from Paris and Boulogne. [My translation.]

It is curious that there is no explicit mention of a trip on the new line itself. Are we to assume that such a trip took place? Or is it conceivable that the party contented itself with a prolonged luncheon at Noyelles?

A second metre gauge line from Noyelles through St Valery to Cayeux, with a station at Lanchères-Pendé, opened two months later on the 6th September (*opposite*). Three possible routes had been considered. The two rejected routes would have taken the railway along the quay and through the town of St Valery, in one case climbing out of the town through Croix-l'Abbé and proceeding to Cayeux via Routhiauville and Sallenelle, and in the other continuing along the coast, past Cap Hornu, and then diverging to serve both Le Hourdel and Cayeux.

In a Convention between the two Companies of the 26th March, the Compagnie du Nord had conceded to the SE the operation of the branch between Noyelles and St Valery, itself undertaking to lay and maintain 'une voie de même écartement que celle de Saint-Valéry à Cayeux' ['a line of the same gauge as that between St Valery and Cayeux']. This agreement was confirmed by Décret on 28th May, and by Résolutions of 10th June and 28th April, 1888. As specified in

Noyelles at Noyelles station. Undated picture postcard.

Noyelles station from the south, showing the metre gauge terminus. Undated picture postcard. The standard gauge main line runs through the station on the other side of the station building on the right.

Another picture postcard of the station at Noyelles.   *Collection R. Arzul*

St. Valery-sur-Somme. Pont de Noyelles à St. Valery (1400 mètres)

The *estacade* between Noyelles and St Valery, with a metre gauge train heading for St Valery and a shepherd with a flock of sheep. Undated picture postcard. *Collection R. Arzul*

A metre gauge train on the *estacade* between Noyelles and St Valery. Undated picture postcard. *Collection R. Arzul*

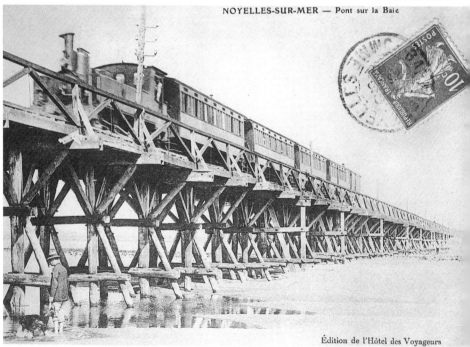

NOYELLES-SUR-MER — Pont sur la Baie

Édition de l'Hôtel des Voyageurs

the agreement, two lines of track, a metre apart, were laid between the standard gauge rails; the reason for doing this, rather than laying a single additional length of track, is likely to have been because of the lighter weight, and differing profile, of the metre gauge rail - the SE utilised Vignole rails of 15 kg/m and 20 kg/m - though it has also been suggested that it was to facilitate the hauling of standard gauge stock by metre gauge locomotives. The agreement was that the SE would take over services on the Noyelles-St Valery line on the date of commencing operations to Cayeux. On that date the Compagnie du Nord ceased to operate passenger trains between Noyelles and St Valery; by the terms of the Convention, the SE undertook to provide its locomotives with a 'double système d'attelage et de tampons' (two sets of couplings and buffers) so that they could deal with standard gauge rolling stock; standard gauge wagons were henceforth hauled by metre gauge locomotives, a practice which continued until 1973 (although a standard gauge locomotive was to be reintroduced to the port of St Valery in World War I and remain there for some years thereafter). The monetary arrangements were somewhat complex, but were based on an established code of practice employed by the CF du Nord elsewhere, by which some costs were shared while the CF du Nord took a portion of receipts up to a defined maximum (1 fr. 50 per train-kilometre). The CF du Nord agreed to take responsibility for the *estacade*, and the SE for the track. The SE agreed to maintain services in the public interest and, in effect, to facilitate connections with Nord trains at Noyelles. The CF du Nord reserved the right to build and maintain locomotives for the SE.

The 'Réseau des Bains de Mer' (preserved in its entirety as today's Chemin de Fer de la Baie de Somme), comprising the two metre-gauge lines heading westwards out of Noyelles, was to become part of the more extensive 'réseau d'intérêt local de la Somme'. However, the 4 km of metre gauge track between Noyelles and St Valery, laid between the standard gauge rails, shared their status as being of *intérêt général*. The nature of this stretch as a branch of the main line was made clear by the type of tickets issued for journeys between Noyelles and St Valery until the closure of the metre gauge line (prior to preservation), and is illustrated to this day by surviving iron kilometre posts marking the distance from Paris. Passengers from Paris, Amiens, and other main line stations could book through to St Valery, but had to purchase separate tickets if changing at Noyelles for Le Crotoy or travelling beyond St Valery to Lanchères or Cayeux. The SNCF (as successor of the Compagnie du Nord) continued to make some use of the standard gauge track until just a few years ago, and owned and maintained the trackbed until 31st December, 1992, when possession passed to the Département.

At St Valery, the existing station alongside the canal continued to be the principal station serving the town; here, on the forecourt, carriages waited to take passengers into the town - the *omnibus pour la ville* charged 30 centimes per person in 1914, plus an additional 30 centimes for luggage not exceeding 30 kilograms. However, the trains to Cayeux also stopped at a halt nearer to the town, where 'les touristes sans bagage' (visitors without luggage) were advised to alight for St Valery. In time the respective status of these two stations would be reversed. A halt at Hurt was authorised by the Prefect in August 1890 in response to representations by local people.

The approach to the original St Valery station, across the lifting bridge over the canal lock. Undated picture postcard. *Collection R. Arzul*

The original St Valery station: the forecourt. Undated picture postcard. *Collection R. Arzul*

The original St Valery station, with the depot on the far side of the tracks: a metre gauge train waiting to depart for Noyelles. Undated picture postcard. *Collection R. Arzul*

St Valery: the 'halt' on the site of the present St Valery Ville station. Undated picture postcard. *Collection R. Arzul*

The station at Cayeux. Undated picture postcard.   *Collection R. Arzul*

The forecourt of the station at Cayeux. Undated picture postcard.   *Collection R. Arzul*

Another view of Cayeux station at around the turn of the century, showing the arrival of a large number of holiday-makers; several horse-drawn vehicles await in the forecourt. Undated picture postcard.   *Collection J-L Rochaix, reproduced with the permision of BVA*

Passengers disembarking at Cayeux. This picture postcard is said to date from 1908.

Collection R. Arzul

CAYEUX SUR MER - L'arrivée du train

B. J. C., Paris

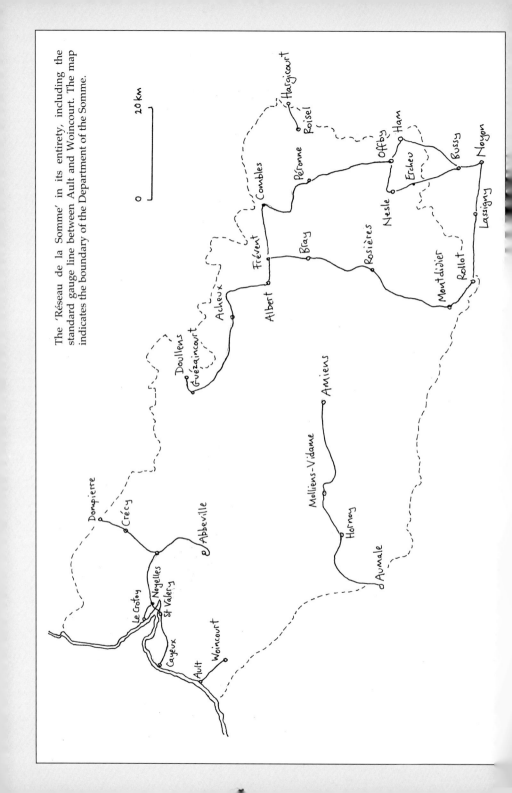

The 'Réseau de la Somme' in its entirety, including the standard gauge line between Ault and Woincourt. The map indicates the boundary of the Department of the Somme.

20 km

In addition to these two lines comprising the 'Réseau des Bains de Mer', a third metre gauge line was constructed from Noyelles; leaving Noyelles, it proceeded north parallel with the main line, gaining height until, curving sharply, it was high enough to cross over the main line on a bridge. It then headed inland to Forest l'Abbaye where it met another metre gauge line from Abbeville; the line continued to Dompierre-sur-Authie. The embanked trackbed can still be seen on both sides of the main line at Noyelles, as can the tiny bridge which carried the railway over the river Dien shortly after it had crossed the main line; further on, entire station buildings remain. The 'Réseau des Bains de Mer' thus formed part of a larger mainly metre-gauge network, including the Noyelles-Forest l'Abbaye and the Abbeville-Dompierre lines, which was itself but part of the 'Réseau de la Somme', by no means all the components of which were physically linked together. To the east, three lines converged on Albert, and a short line linked Roisel and Hargicourt. Another line proceeded westwards from Amiens to Aumale. Not far south of Cayeux, a standard gauge line from Ault, on the coast, to Woincourt, partly following the course of an earlier narrow gauge tramway, opened before World War I by a company formed in 1903 for this purpose (the Compagnie des Chemins de fer Industriels et Balnéaires de la Somme) was to become part of the SE's 'Réseau de la Somme' after the war. (It is interesting to note that the Compagnie des CF Industriels et Balnéaires also considered the possibility of building a line from Le Tréport to Cayeux via Boise-de Cise, la Croix-au-Bailly, and Ault-Onival.) All of these added up to some 340 km, of which the 'Réseau des Bains de Mer' represented just 19 km (*opposite*).

Motive power throughout the SE's Somme network was provided almost exclusively by 0-6-2T locomotives, from various manufacturers, of between 19.5 and 21.5 tons (empty) and 24.5 and 33.5 tons (loaded) (*see page 46*); they are listed in Appendix One. Locomotives were stationed at depots at Abbeville, Amiens, St Roch, and, St Valery, and on the distinct Albert network, at the principal depot at Albert and also at Acheux, Bussy, Doullens, Ercheu, Fricourt, Ham, Montdidier, Nesle, Péronne and Rosières. While it is evident that locomotives were moved within the network as a whole, it would appear that some 10 locomotives were stationed at St Valery - at least, 10 were noted (in a report by the Département's Ingénieur Ordinaire des Mines dated 23rd January, 1897) to have been based at St Valery in the previous year - Nos. 3.519, 3.520, 3.521, 3.522, 3.523, 3.524, 3.530, 3.535, 3.540, and 3.564 - though one of these, No. 3.530, had been sent to the Albert network on 13th November. The following locomotives are additionally known from photographic evidence to have worked on the Réseau des Bains de Mer: 3.526, 3.537, 3.561, 3.615, 3.661. All are recorded by Guy Pérève as having been based at St Valery at some time except No. 3.537. In addition, Nos. 3.528, 3.563, 3.565, 3.566, 3.567, 3.569, 3.571, 3.510 and 3.512 are also recorded by Guy Pérève as having been based for all or part of their time on the Somme network at St Valery. Running repairs were undertaken at the depot at St Valery; for more substantial repairs, locomotives from the 'Réseau des Bains de Mer' were taken to Albert on standard gauge wagons via the CF du Nord.

Metre gauge steam locomotives which worked on the 'Réseau des Bains de Mer' were generally fitted with twin buffers as well as a centre buffer, to enable them to couple on to standard gauge rolling stock on the mixed gauge section between Noyelles and St Valery.

The halt at Morlay on the Le Crotoy line.   *Collection R. Arzul*

Le Crotoy station. Undated picture postcard.   *Collection R. Arzul*

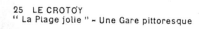

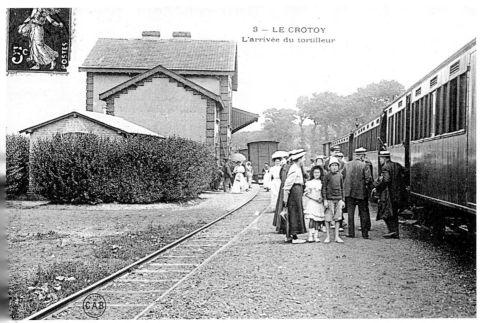

3 – LE CROTOY
L'arrivée du tortilleur

Le Crotoy station. Undated picture postcard.   *Collection R. Arzul*

The departure of a train from Le Crotoy. This picture postcard is said to date from 1910.
Collection R. Arzul

LE CROTOY - Le Tortillard

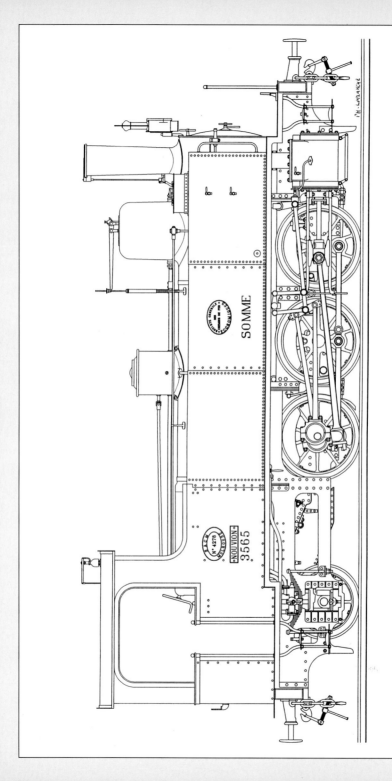

S.E. SOMME .031T SACM TYPE 66

SACM 0-6-2T locomotive type 66, as used by the SE on its Somme network. Drawing by P.H. Laplanche; reproduced with thanks to G. Laplanche and Keith Clingan.

Passenger traffic

From the outset, the 'Réseau des Bains de Mer' carried significant numbers of holiday-makers in the summer, for St Valery and the resorts of Le Crotoy and Cayeux had become popular holiday haunts for people living in northern France and the Paris region. In 1896, in addition to the original coaches (built by Desouches & David, and by Decauville) two *fourgons* - baggage vans intended specifically for use in passenger trains - were fitted out to carry passengers during peak periods on the Cayeux line! The population of these three towns multiplied by five or six between mid-June and mid-September. During the 'Saison des Bains de Mer', the Compagnie du Nord offered bargain fares to these and other seaside resorts, including season tickets intended for families, weekly tickets, and 'excursion' tickets. In 1914 a 3rd class excursion from Paris to St Valery cost 6 francs 5 centimes, or would have done so had the war not intervened. Some families took lodgings for weeks at a time, their menfolk joining them at weekends; it would seem that during the week some wives took full advantage of their husbands' absence, for the Friday evening train from Paris became known as the 'train des cocus' (the cuckolds' train)! Some 45,000 railway tickets to Cayeux were sold in 1903, a figure which rose to around 70,000 by 1911.

The *Guide Baedeker* of 1893 quotes the following fares from Noyelles:

	1st class	2nd class	3rd class
St Valery Gare	70	55	35
Cayeux	2.05	1.60	1.10
Le Crotoy	90	70	50

Although holiday-makers are encouraged to travel by train to reach their holiday destination, the idea of using the railway to take a trip round the Bay had not yet taken hold. Between the towns of St Valery and Le Crotoy, on opposite sides of the Bay, 'Par la chemin de fer, il y a 14 kil. et les trains ne correspondent guère' ('The distance is 14 kil. and the trains seldom connect'). Instead, direct crossings of the Bay are recommended; at low tide by boat (across the river) and on foot, and at high tide by boat all the way for 60 centimes.

Timetables dating from the opening of the metre gauge lines in 1887 show four trains per day in each direction between Noyelles and Le Crotoy, five trains per day between Noyelles, St Valery and Cayeux, and an additional four trains between Noyelles and St Valery only. The January 1903 timetable shows three trains each day operating from Cayeux and from Le Crotoy through to Noyelles, with two trains returning in each case. A rather more frequent service operated between St Valery and Noyelles, with five trains from St Valery in addition to the through trains from Cayeux. A 3.30 am departure from Noyelles to St Valery facilitated an overnight journey from Paris. A pattern of more or less simultaneous arrivals and departures at Noyelles which has remained a feature of operations ever since is evident, providing connections with main line trains to and from Amiens and Paris. Trains arrive from Le Crotoy and

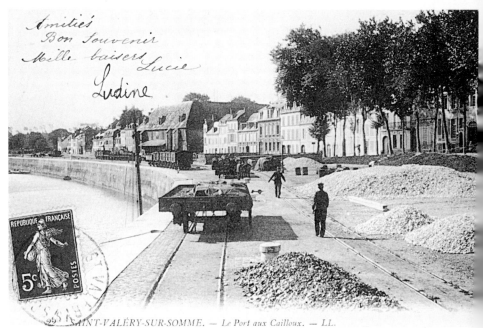

St Valery quay looking east; standard gauge and metre gauge track, a standard gauge wagon, and heaps of *galets*. The salt warehouse is visible, complete with the roof which was demolished in 1900. Undated picture postcard. *Collection R. Arzul*

St Valery quay, looking west. The salt warehouse, complete with roof (which dates this picture postcard before 1900) is on the left. From the centre to the right, standard gauge, metre gauge, and standard gauge tracks, with trucks standing on the latter. Note the perambulator being pushed between the metre gauge rails. *Collection Philip Pacey*

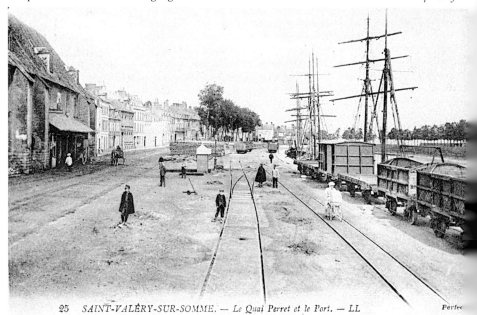

Cayeux at 6.32 and 6.34 am, at 10.37 and 10.40 am, and at 6.00 and 6.05 in the afternoon; trains depart from Noyelles at 8.09 and 8.10 am, and at 4.10 and 4.12 pm. The May 1914 timetable not surprisingly shows rather more trains operating, with four daily return journeys between Cayeux and Noyelles and Le Crotoy and Noyelles, and seven additional trains from St Valery to Noyelles (with six return journeys). Interestingly, the 3.30 am departure from Noyelles was still in place, and was still scheduled to arrive at St Valery at 3.42.

Goods Traffic

Before the railway came, the port of St Valery handled *galets* (flint, or silica, pebbles), brought on flat barges, or rafts, from Cayeux, around the point of Le Hourdel to the quay at St Valery, where they were transferred to ships and, possibly, canal barges, and to trains when the railway arrived at St Valery. Transporting *galets* from Cayeux by raft was a perilous process; the slightest wind caused problems: on 29th April, 1882 12 rafts, with more than 200 people aboard, were wrecked in the mouth of the Bay. The *galets* found in quantity around Cayeux are said to be exceptionally pure. *Galets* served many uses: as a building material; as aggregate in concrete; in various grinding, pounding, and pulverising processes; and, broken and powdered, in special sands and abrasives and in the ceramics industry (notably as a constituent of *faïence*). Other goods which passed through the port, increasingly so after it became connected to the rail network and began to compete with Boulogne and Le Tréport, included timber, jute, textiles, soap, coal, and phosphates. Phosphates were extracted at Crécy en Ponthieu, so were easily transported by metre gauge train when the Réseau de Somme was extended in this direction, east of Noyelles.

Some indication of the range and quantity of goods shipped from the Baie de Somme is contained in a fascinating document dating from 1893 which survives in the Archives at Amiens, a proposal from a local ship owner, M. de Raesfeld, for a 600 mm gauge Decauville tramway, using steam locomotives, linking the harbour at Le Hourdel with the railway on the quay at St Valery. De Raesfeld favoured Le Hourdel over St Valery because of the greater depth of water in the harbour; he envisaged his tramway following the edge of the coast from Le Hourdel to the base of William's tower at St Valery, then continuing along what is now the promenade at St Valery, running alongside the tracks on the quay, and continuing to end on the south side of the lock opposite St Valery Canal. He estimated the likely annual traffic to be:

Coal	12,000 tons	108,000 francs
Phosphates	15,000 tons	105,000 francs
Sugarbeet	15,000 tons	112,500 francs
Silex (*galets*)	5,000 tons	37,500 francs
Quartzites	3,000 tons	13,500 francs

Galets continued to be brought to St Valery by sea until the metre gauge railway was extended to Cayeux; after that the hazardous barge journeys were abandoned

SAINT-VALÉRY-SUR-SOMME
Le Port — Arrivée d'un voilier

Edition de la Ruche Picarde

The arrival of a sailing ship at the port of St Valery, seen from a little further up the quay, still looking west. The standard gauge track to the left can be seen to cross the metre gauge track. Undated picture postcard.   *Collection R. Arzul*

A bit further along the quay. In this view the former harbour-master's office, just visible in the picture postcard of the sailing ship, is seen to the right. Today this building has found a new lease of life as an information centre for visitors. Note the heap of flint pebbles (*galets*).The barrels may well contain wine.   *Collection R. Arzul*

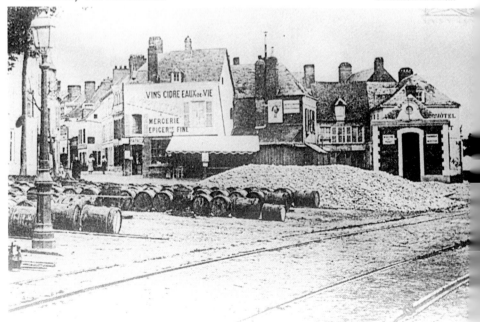

Temporary track and horse-drawn skip wagons being used for gathering *galets* from the beach at Brighton (north of Cayeux). 600 mm track was used for transporting *galets* from the beach to rafts, or to ships at the quay at Le Hourdel, or to the station at Cayeux to be transferred to metre gauge wagons, and to nearby crushing plants.   *Collection R. Arzul*

Gathering *galets* at Cayeux.   *Collection R. Arzul*

Gathering *galets* at Cayeux.   *Collection R. Arzul*

The 600 mm track for transporting *galets*, passing by L'Ecce Homo, a roadside shrine, at Cayeux.
Collection R. Arzul

«Le Hourdel»— Quai Médard

Skip wagons on the pier at Le Hourdel.   *Collection R. Arzul*

The pier at Le Hourdel. In this view, an unidentified steam locomotive can just be discerned among the skips wagons on the pier (*to the left of centre*).   *Collection R. Arzul*

47. - CAYEUX-sur-MER. - Chargement des Galets au Hourdel

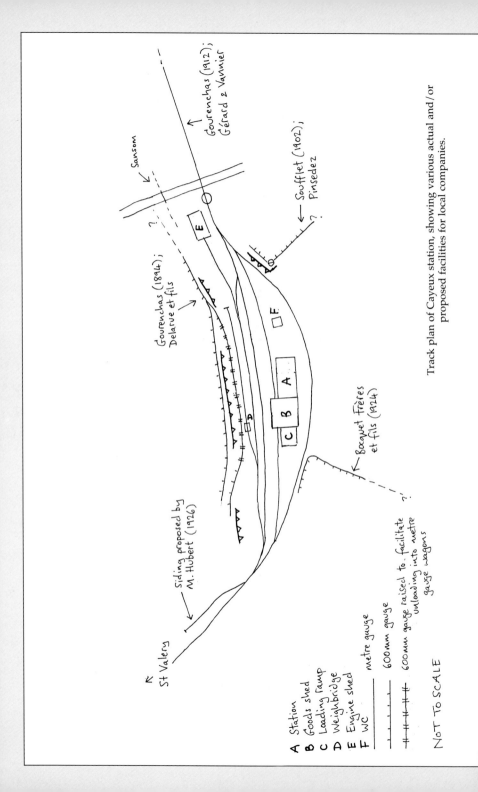

St Valéry

Siding proposed by
M. Hubert (1926)

Sansom

Gourenchas (1894);
Delarue et fils

Gourenchas (1912);
Gérard 2 Vannier

Soufflet (1902);
Pinsedez
?

Bocquet Frères
et fils (1924)

?'
600mm gauge raised to facilitate
unloading into metre
gauge wagons

A Station
B Goods shed
C Loading ramp
D Weighbridge
E Engine shed
F WC

——————— metre gauge
—————— 600mm gauge
-H-H-H-H- 600mm gauge raised to facilitate unloading into metre gauge wagons

NOT TO SCALE

Track plan of Cayeux station, showing various actual and/or
proposed facilities for local companies.

in favour of transportation by rail (although some internal CF du Nord correspondence regarding the future of the ports of Abbeville, Le Hourdel and St Valery, dating from 1919, indicates that a M. Medard had at that time only relatively recently stopped shipping *galets* from Le Hourdel to St Valery by motorised barge; an extension of the railway from Cayeux to Le Hourdel is suggested as a more practical alternative to maintaining Le Hourdel as anything more than a 'port de refuge'). Portable Decauville track had been used for some time for transporting *galets* from the beach ; now, after the metre gauge railway had reached Cayeux, 500 mm and 600 mm Decauville tramways were at various times laid along certain roads around and through the town to the station yard; here they were raised on embankments or by other means to facilitate transhipment of the *galets* to metre gauge wagons. In 1912 the metre gauge line was extended beyond the turntable, across the road, and for some 54 metres, to meet a 500 mm or 600 mm gauge tramway from the 'exploitation des galets' then owned by Messrs Gourenchas et Cie (later sold to Messrs Gérard & Vannier). The remains of another metre gauge branch crossing the road at another point can still be seen; this line, which served the Sansom factory just beyond the road, may not have been installed until after World War II and was still in use in the 1960s (*see opposite*).

Two crops grown locally were served by the railway; interestingly, both had become established in France in part as a result of Napoleon's determination, announced in 1811, to free France from dependence on the British colonies, and of 'tit for tat' attempts by the French to close Europe to British shipping and by the British to blockade French ports. Chicory was grown and marketed as an alternative to imported coffee; sugar beet was cultivated as an alternative to importing sugar cane*. Sugar beet was invariably processed in the regions in which it was grown, because the weight of the roots made transporting them expensive; light railway systems were often used to carry the roots to nearby *raperies* where they were shredded; the shredded beet was then transferred, sometimes from several *raperies*, and in some cases, as with the *raperie* at Lanchères, by being washed down a pipeline, to a *sucrerie* where the juice was extracted, refined, and reduced to white sugar; the pulp was used as animal feed. Between October and January (thus, nicely complementing the holiday season) sugar beet grown near the Baie de Somme was carried on the metre gauge railway. Some was taken to a *raperie* at Crécy, some to the *raperie* at Lanchères, between St Valery and Cayeux. At Le Crotoy the loading of sugar beet onto railway wagons, and the unloading of sugar beet pulp, in the station yard ('in front of the WC') eventually (in 1929) was felt to detract from the service to passengers to such an extent that the track layout was altered, by lengthening the loop line around the station building, to enable more wagons to be loaded or unloaded at a time, but further away from the station itself. During the sugar beet season in 1928, some 769 ten-ton wagons had been loaded or unloaded at Le Crotoy, including 470 wagonloads of outgoing sugar beet roots, and 109 wagonloads of incoming sugar beet pulp.

*A method for extracting sugar from beet had been discovered by a Prussian chemist in 1747 but its development did not progress very far until, spurred on by Napoleon's urgings, Benjamin Delessert developed a working sugar beet factory; he was rewarded by Napoleon in 1812. In the next year 300 factories were established. The French sugar beet industry collapsed when trade between France and Britain resumed in 1814 and West Indian sugar was again imported, but it recovered in the 1840s and has flourished ever since. To this day, most of mainland Europe's sugar is produced from sugar beet, while British sugar comes from sugar cane.

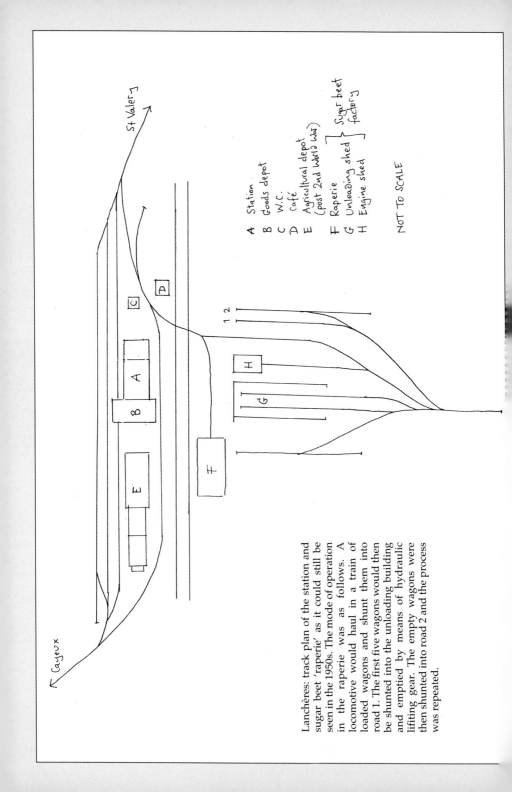

Cayeux

St Valery

A Station
B Goods depot
C W.C.
D Café
E Agricultural depot (post 2nd World War)
F Raperie
G Unloading shed } Sugar beet factory
H Engine shed

NOT TO SCALE

Lanchères: track plan of the station and sugar beet 'raperie' as it could still be seen in the 1950s. The mode of operation in the raperie was as follows. A locomotive would haul in a train of loaded wagons and shunt them into road 1. The first five wagons would then be shunted into the unloading building and emptied by means of hydraulic lifiting gear. The empty wagons were then shunted into road 2 and the process was repeated.

In spite of being quite small, the *raperie* at Lanchères, latterly owned by the Société F. Béghin, laid its own metre gauge railway network (*opposite*) and eventually acquired two steam locomotives, Corpet Louvet 0-6-0T *La Scarpe* (1087/1907) and an Orenstein & Koppel 0-6-0T (8084/1911); while it is not known when the refinery began operations or established its railway system or acquired its first locomotive, records survive of a request, made in 1904, by the Compagnie Sucrière de la Somme, for a branch line to be constructed at Lanchères. *La Scarpe* was not acquired until 1951; the Orenstein & Koppel, originally a 770 mm gauge locomotive delivered new to Festungs Eb. Baukompanie 8, Grandfontaine, may have been in sole charge for some time before this. In addition to shunting duties at Lanchères these locomotives sometimes travelled from Lanchères to and even beyond Noyelles at the head of the sugar beet trains.

The railway also served a chicory processing factory, situated between the line and the canal at St Valery, close to the original station and later halt; the derelict factory building survived until 1998 (*see page 60*), when it was deemed to be unsafe to leave standing; it contained a 600 mm tramway, used, it is thought, for carrying fuel to, and ashes from, the furnaces which heated ovens in which chicory roots were roasted. The owner of the chicory factory, Alexandre Humbert, asked in 1926 for a siding at Cayeux for loading chicory roots grown locally, and in 1929 for the siding which was built to serve the factory at St Valery Canal (and which partially survives, complete with weigh-bridge).

Other freight carried by the railway included shellfish. While local shellfish were taken from the Bay, in some cases for sale in Abbeville market, some other types of shellfish which were not available locally were (but from what date?) brought in the opposite direction, to be served (if nowhere else) in the Madot restaurant at Le Crotoy which continued to make use of the railway until its closure. In 1907 a M. Coustre Victor proposed laying a 500 mm Decauville tramway from oysterbeds in the bay beyond the western end of the present-day promenade at St Valery; it is not clear whether this tramway was ever laid and used. It was intended that the tramway would be laid along the sea-front, the length of the present Le Romerel promenade and onto the quay, ending in an exchange siding alongside the existing railway.

* * * * * * *

The long wooden viaduct or *estacade* between Noyelles and St Valery must have provided a good deal of excitement for passengers, especially at very high tides when the structure was all but entirely submerged. It seems that in certain conditions, when a strong wind was blowing from the north-west, it was considered less of a risk to insist that passengers should get out of the train and cross the 1,300 metre viaduct on foot, rejoining the train on the other side; if it had been blown off, it would not have taken them with it! Following the construction of the trestle viaduct across the Bay, Dr Eugène Lomier wrote 'the idea naturally arose of doubling its width to accommodate a road suitable for road vehicles and pedestrians, to cut the distance from St-Valery to Noyelles' [my translation]. A proposal to this effect which he presented to the Conseil municipal on 8th June, 1908 was apparently favourably received; although his suggestion wasn't

Corpet-Louvet 0-6-0T No. 24 *La Scarpe* approaching the *raperie* at Lanchères with a train of sugar beet. Lanchères station is in the background.   *Collection R. Arzul*

The *raperie* at Lanchères, looking into the loading shed. Corpet-Louvet 0-6-0T No. 24 *La Scarpe* is coming off the shed road.   *Collection R. Arzul*

The Orenstein & Koppel 0-6-0T at the *raperie* at Lanchères. *Collection R. Arzul*

Corpet-Louvet 0-6-0T No. 24 *La Scarpe* at the *raperie* at Lanchères in October 1960.
B. Rozè, reproduced with the permission of BVA

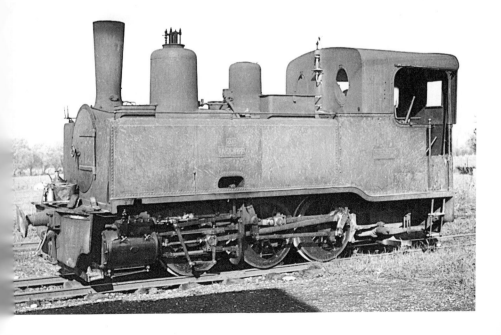

implemented (a new road between St Valery and Noyelles, following a less adventurous route, was built in 1912), he later felt that his belief in the value of the crossing was vindicated by the use made of it during World War I. In 1910 and 1911 the *estacade* - which according to some sources was by this time in poor condition due to its constant immersion in water - was replaced by a solid embankment. Just a few years later the embankment was widened, and put to a surprising use; that story will be told in the chapter which follows.

In 1886, prior to its construction, the Conseil Municipal de Cayeux had asked for the Cayeux line to be standard gauge, and in 1911 they repeated the request, at the same time asking for the station at Cayeux to be 'aggrandised'. The SE's response was to dismiss the former, but to encourage the latter, especially if the town could contribute to the costs. An interesting feature of the plans, drawn up by local architect L. Käppler and preserved in the Archives at Amiens, is the intended complete separation of passenger and freight activities on different sides of the tracks, with the 'aggrandised' station building being given over exclusively to passengers. This would have represented a radical departure from normal practice on French country railways, and it surely reflects the importance of both functions at Cayeux - the holiday-makers, on the one hand, providing a vital contribution to the local economy; the range and quantity of goods on the other. (The *halle aux marchandises* had previously been enlarged with the addition of a second enclosed loading bay following proposals drawn up in 1894.) M. Käppler noted growth in the number of passengers (some 70,000 per annum), in the *trafic des messageries* (parcels), and in the transportation of sugar beet (700 10-ton wagon loads per season) and of *galets* (10,000 tons per annum). The station had still not been rebuilt in 1914, when, in January, posters announced a public enquiry into proposals to fund it by means of temporary local *surtaxes*; perhaps this did not go down too well - and of course the war intervened - since the reconstruction was destined never to take place.

The chicory factory close to St Valery Canal, shortly before its demolition in 1998. In this view, the railway lies on the other side of the building, and the canal is off the picture to the left; the gantry over the road would have been used for loading barges. *Philip Pacey*

Chapter Four

The 'Réseau des Bains de Mer' during World War I

During the afternoon of 19th August, 1914, five trains in succession, carrying the 11th English artillery regiment, stopped at Noyelles. People from round about, including some from St Valery, brought apples, biscuits, bread, beer, tobacco and cigarettes for the troops. Eugène Lomier, a local doctor who recorded this memory, also recalled that, towards the end of 1914,

> ... on percevait très distinctement de Saint-Valery, surtout pendant la nuit, les coups de sifflet avertisseurs ainsi que le roulement des trains qui se suivaient sans interruptions, sur la ligne du chemin de fer du Nord, vers Rue, de l'autre côte de la Baie.

That is, people in St Valery could hear, very distinctly (and especially at night), the whistling of trains from across the Bay, as train followed train without interruption on the main line.

While many thousands of troops passed through Noyelles during the war, for nearly 900 Chinese recruited by the British army it became their last resting place. Chinese personnel were stationed here from the spring of 1916; their presence clearly intrigued a teenage witness of events, Joseph de Valicourt, who noted how they used baskets on the ends of bamboo poles to carry things, including ash from locomotives at Noyelles; the ash was used by the British troops in the area to make roads in their camps, as a constituent of concrete, and even to make tennis courts (including one in the De Valicourt family garden, close to Noyelles station). While up to 90,000 Chinese may have been deployed at Noyelles in the course of the war, the 900 destined not to leave were the victims of an epidemic; they are buried in the 'Cimitière chinois' at nearby Nolette.

Thanks to W.J.K. Davies and others, the role of railways in supporting the Western Front is generally well known. In the first four months of the war, the German forces advanced menacingly but were held not far short of Paris; German and Allied forces then extended their fronts northwards to the Channel coast, each hoping to outflank the other, and thus the Western Front was established. The Allies were able to make use of the Calais-Boulogne-Amiens-Paris main line and various other standard gauge and metre gauge lines to transport supplies to railheads short of the Front (*see page 62*); from these railheads, temporary 600 mm gauge tracks were laid to the Front itself, the initiative being taken by the French with much of their equipment being initially supplied by Decauville Aîné. The British authorities took rather longer to be convinced either that trench warfare would be prolonged or that light railways were essential. They became persuaded partly by 'home-made' tramways improvised on the ground, partly as a result of taking over a sector of the front line, fully equipped with light railway systems, from the French 10th Army early in 1916, and partly through the bitter experience of the Somme offensive which, by default, demonstrated the need for efficient transportation of large quantities of supplies from main railheads to the scene of action.

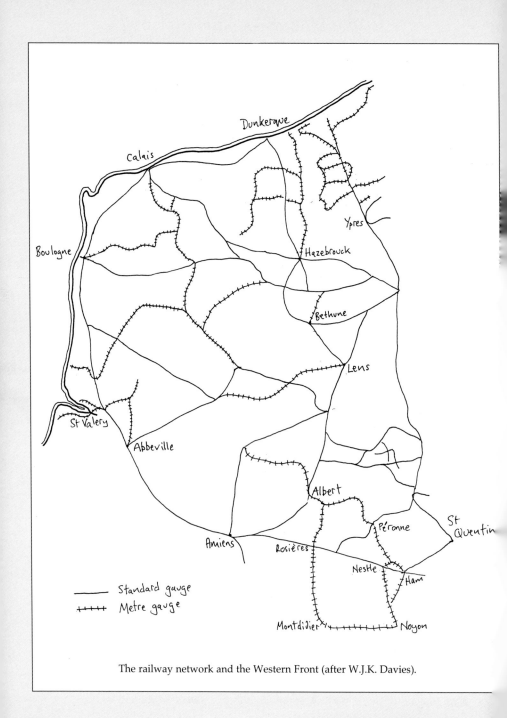

The railway network and the Western Front (after W.J.K. Davies).

The main ports to which supplies were shipped were Dunkirk, Calais and Boulogne. Smaller but significant, and increasing, quantities of supplies were also landed at the port of St Valery, which was conceded to the British Admiralty, as the following figures show:

	Ships	Capacity (tons)
1914 (from 1st August)	10	995
1915	23	1,532
1916	217	36,992
1917	502	109,333
1918	528	85,244

Colonel Henniker's study, *Transportation on the Western Front 1914-1918*, includes a table of 'estimated weekly tonnage to be discharged at ports in France for the offensive of 1917' which gives the following breakdown for St Valery:

	2,000 tons forage
	300 tons general supplies
	400 tons Expeditionary Force canteens
Total	2,700 tons

This compares to 32,000 tons at Dunkirk, and is the lowest total of the 10 ports shown. Another table, showing 'Allocation to ports of estimated weekly dead weight tonnage. Revised for month of February 1917' indicates 1,940 tons of 'supplies' against St Valery, as compared to more than 20,000 at each of Dunkirk, Calais and Le Havre, 36,000 at Boulogne, 42,600 at Rouen, but only 1,000 at Fécamp and a mere 135 at Le Tréport. Detailed information regarding how much of the material landed at St Valery was carried forward by which means of transport is lacking, but the fact that the British army ripped out the metre gauge tracks on the quay and made use of a standard gauge locomotive hired from the CF du Nord demonstrates that standard gauge wagons were preferred to metre gauge stock. Use was also made of the Somme canal which passed beside a large depot at Saigneville, to which a short standard gauge branch line was built from the Abbeville-Le Tréport line. According to Dr Lomier the railway embankment between St Valery and Noyelles facilitated the movement of troops, being crossed 'almost daily' by detachments of the British army; British troops also 'came close to using it to retreat towards Normandy, in the face of the advance of the Germans towards Amiens in the spring of 1918'.

The Noyelles-St Valery railway became peculiarly involved in the war following the German offensive which began on 21st March, 1918 and which broke the stalemate of trench warfare. On 21st March the Germans attacked along the front between Arras and Tergnier. (During that night the ammunition depot at Saigneville was bombed; Joseph de Valicourt, at Noyelles, saw the whole sky lit up and the countryside illuminated by red light, followed by explosions and flarings-up of different colours - red, green, and yellow.) The British 5th Army, which had taken over this sector only a few weeks earlier, was overrun and thrust back towards Amiens. A new defence line, constructed by troops hastily brought by rail, held; a second German offensive, in April,

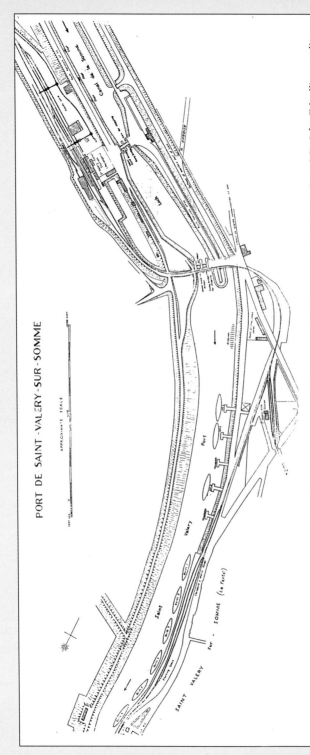

PORT DE SAINT - VALÉRY - SUR - SOMME

APPROXIMATE SCALE

St Valery. This plan is British in origin, and although there is evidence which suggests that it was issued (by Vice-Admiral Sir John Edgell) no earlier than 1938, it appears to represent the situation early in World War I and to indicate British interest in the capacity of the port of St Valery at that time. Although no distinction is made between track of different gauges, track on the quay is indicated to be 'standard and metre gauge'; the British removed the metre gauge track from the quay during the war, and it was not reinstated until several years afterwards. Although St Valery Ville is so named, and is called a 'station' rather than a 'halt', the original station buildings are shown at St Valery (Canal). Is this, then, a map from World War I which was re-issued in World War II?

achieved some success further north before the front stabilised once more with neither side being able to take advantage of the other's exhaustion - that is, until the Allies began to advance in August. It was during this time (in late April, following the destructive attack on Saigneville) that ammunition dumps were established 'at stations on the Noyelles-Dompierre metre gauge line' (Henniker p. 412).

A special train, comprising a locomotive and two *wagon-lits* of the Compagnie du Chemin de fer du Nord, had spent the night of 2nd-3rd March, 1918, at the port of St Valery. Its occupants included M. Javary, Chef d'exploitation de la Compagnie, and an 'état-major d'ingénieurs mobilisés' - or in other words, the Commission de Réseau du Nord (one of several such Commissions, each comprising one military and one professional railway person, together responsible for the working relationship between military and railway authorities). The reason for their visit was not disclosed, but within a few weeks St Valery was to be the scene of part of a remarkable feat of engineering. Another 'train mystérieux' arrived towards 6.00 on the evening of 2nd May. The following day rumours spread that on the train were the President of the Republic, Poincaré, and the President of Conseil, Clemenceau, and that evening, when the occupants went on foot to dine at the hotel 'A la Colonne de Bronze', a curious crowd gathered. In fact, Eugène Lomier implies, the visitation was a sign of the removal to St Valery - in response to the same military crisis which had provoked the decision to build a new railway line - of the Commission de Réseau du Nord. They set up their temporary headquarters in the old Hôtel de France, rue de la Ferté.

The pressing military circumstances were these. When the German advance simultaneously called for the movement of troops and supplies, *and* threatened the main line through Amiens, the principal means of bringing those troops to where they were needed, the Commission de Réseau du Nord was asked to advise on the viability of alternative routes. Options included improvement of existing railway lines including doubling the Dieppe-Eu, Longroy-Longpré, and Abbeville-St Riquier lines; quadrupling the main line north from Port le Grand (south of Noyelles) to Etaples, doubling some lines and improving other, single, lines, in the triangle Abancourt-Rouen-Beauvais. But these works by themselves would only allow for the transit of 60-70 trains per day, less than the capacity of the main line. So it was proposed that a largely new two-track standard gauge route should be built to link the main line from Calais and Boulogne with the Abancourt-St Omer line. General Foch asked military and civilian engineers how long the construction of such a line would take; the former suggested 18 months, but Raoul Dautry*, an engineer with the Compagnie du Chemin de Fer du Nord, said it could be done in 100 days. It seems he was inspired by an entry in Flaubert's *Dictionnaire des idées reçues*:

---

*Raoul Dautry may be an unfamiliar name to English readers, but he is something of a hero in his native France. He worked for the CF du Nord from 1903 to 1928; then he was successively Director General of the CF de l'Etat (1928-1937), Minister of Armaments (1939-40), Minister of Reconstruction and Town Planning (1944-46) and General Administrator of the Commissariat for Atomic Energy (1946-51), a record of achievement which led to him being described as 'l'un des artisans de la modernisation de la France'.

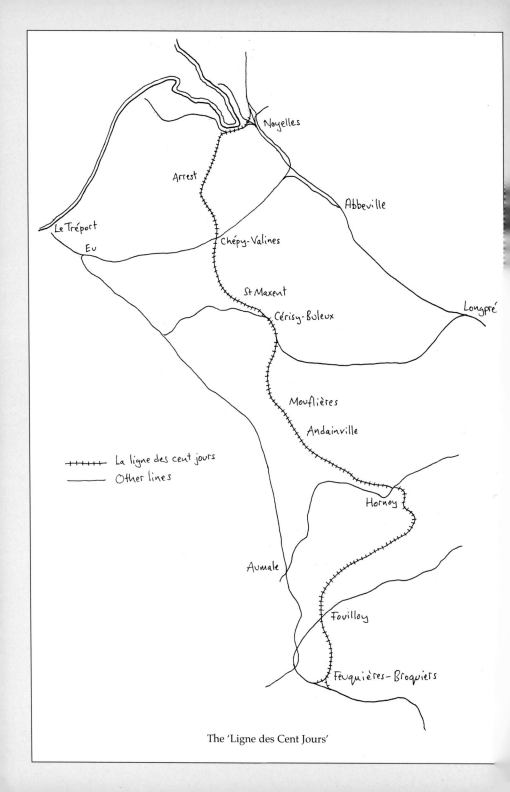

The 'Ligne des Cent Jours'

Chemins de fer. Si Napoléon les avait eus à sa disposition, il aurait été invincible. ['If Napoleon had had railways at his disposal, he would have been invincible'].

Dautry was put in charge of the project on 1st May; work began on the ground on the 15th. Dautry was given a labour force of some 20,000 men including 8,500 miners whose primary task was the digging of a second tunnel at Marseille-en-Beauvaisis. Dr Lomier noted that a detachment of troops came to St Valery to work on the line. 'We remember Dr Lemoine, doctor to this detachment, to whom we paid many visits in his 'wagon' which was located near the station-master's house'. (The latter, now no more, was close to the original St Valery station, subsequently the St Valery Canal halt, between it and the chicory factory.) There is no evidence that the Chinese stationed at Noyelles were involved in the construction of the 'ligne de cent jours'; one wonders if they were involved in other railway construction work nearby - there was plenty going on.

The 'ligne des cent jours' left the main line at Ponthoile, just north of Noyelles; its route will be described shortly. Here at Ponthoile, a number of sidings were installed on the western side of the main line, as was an 'atelier de contrôle et de changement de roues pour les wagons'. The 'ligne des cent jours' diverged from the main line on this same side; on the other side, the new trackbed laid as part of the quadrupling of the main line diverged from the established route's approach to Noyelles at this same point; after crossing the metre gauge line to Forest l'Abbaye just after this line had passed over the main line, it bent back towards the main line, heading straight for Noyelles and in fact squeezing past two houses near the level crossing at Noyelles to run parallel with the main line once again. It would appear that, rather than simply rejoining the established main line, a continuation of this line gained height to cross the main line and the Somme canal at Port-le-Grand, joining the line from Abbeville to Le Tréport and thence linking with the 'ligne de cent jours' at Chépy. This complex of established and strategic lines was thus to provide various options while significantly increasing the capacity for north-south traffic. The route of this line through the meadows at Noyelles can be seen very clearly on aerial photographs taken during World War II (*see page 89*); indeed, some signs can still be seen on the ground, and on large scale maps, to this day. Joseph de Valicourt observes that by diverging from the main line at Ponthoile (he refers to a 'new station called Ponthoile-Mollière') both of these lines avoided the railway junction of Noyelles and indeed bypassed the bridge carrying the metre gauge line over the main line which the Germans succeeded in destroying in August 1944, briefly (one assumes) disrupting traffic on the main line and halting trains on the metre gauge line for six weeks.

As for the celebrated 'ligne de cent jours' itself: on diverging from the *west* side of the main line at Ponthoile, it curved sharply away through the fields to join the existing mixed gauge line between Noyelles and St Valery. Adopting this single line, it added a second standard gauge line, an enterprise which involved widening the embankment across the head of the bay. Having crossed the bay, the new route struck off on its own to the west of St Valery, at the point where the line to St Valery, still on its embankment, bends east towards St

THE SOMME CROSSINGS WEST OF AMIENS,
MARCH, 1918.

SKETCH 14.

THE FIGURES SHOW THE ESTIMATED MAXIMUM NUMBER OF TRAIN MOVEMENTS POSSIBLE DAILY IN EACH DIRECTION.

The capacity of the railway network west of Amiens in March, 1918. From Colonel Henniker's *Transportation on the Western Front 1914-1918.*

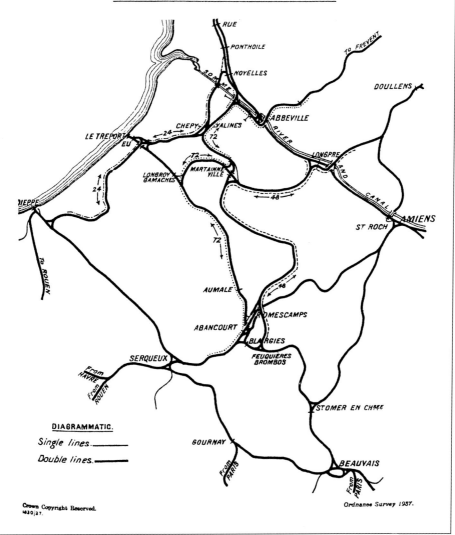

SKETCH 15.

THE SOMME CROSSINGS WEST OF AMIENS, AUGUST. 1918.

SHOWING THREE INDEPENDENT ROUTES, WITH THE NUMBER OF TRAIN MOVEMENTS POSSIBLE DAILY IN EACH DIRECTION OVER EACH.

The capacity of the railway network west of Amiens in August, 1918, following construction of the 'Ligne des Cent Jours', the construction of some other lines, and the doubling of some existing single track lines. From Colonel Henniker's *Transportation on the Western Front 1914-1918.*

Valery Canal, and continued to Feuquière-Broquiers, a length of some 88 km. (This compares to 62 km as the crow flies, a difference accounted for by the necessity to avoid major civil engineering work by following the lie of the land) (*see page 66*).

Track was laid, by and large, by 15th July. Work was largely completed by 1st August, and the line was opened by President Georges Clemenceau in a ceremony at Marseille-le-Petit on 15th August at which Raoul Dautry was made Chevalier of the Légion d'Honneur. Colonel Henniker observes:

> This line is a noteworthy example of railway construction in war-time, notable alike for the completeness of the design, the magnitude of the work and the rapidity of its execution. A trunk line complete with engine sheds, water supplies, signalling, telephones, station buildings, etc., had been constructed in 131 days from the date when its construction was first contemplated, or 106 days from the date on which work started on the ground.

Henniker's study *Transportation on the Western Front* includes two maps illustrating the situation before and after the construction of the line and the completion of other works, and indicating the maximum number of train movements possible daily in each direction on each line (*see pages 68 & 69*).

It is sometimes suggested that the line was never used, except by the many works trains which assisted in its construction. According to Henniker, the line was 'first used for a strategical [*sic*] troop movement early in October [when the French Sixth Army was being moved to Flanders prior to mounting an attack on October 14th] and then only as a supplement to the two *rocade* lines passing through Longueau...' It ceased to be used on 1st January, 1919, and the track was lifted in March and April 1919, though not before proposals had been put forward by the Chambre de Commerce d'Abbeville for retaining the line as a relief route for holiday traffic from Paris. The route of the line shows up clearly on aerial photographs taken from Allied reconnaissance aircraft scarcely 20 years later. Remains can still be seen near St Valery, in addition to the widened embankment; at the point where it left the mixed gauge line, a piece of concrete in the undergrowth of the embankment may have been the abutment of a bridge which carried the line across the road; on the far side of the road, trackbed can be discerned in the field; a raised cross-section of trackbed is apparent in the further river bank and two lines of trackbed are clearly visible crossing this next field (aerial photos show that the double tracks separated shortly after leaving the metre gauge line, running parallel but at a distance on both sides of the river - which would have been crossed by two bridges - and then converging again); a few metres further on, near Drancourt, a cutting is very obvious, and no doubt other signs remain elsewhere.

Chapter Five

The 'Réseau des Bains de Mer' From 1918 to 1939

'Why must we be beholden to our enemies for demonstrating the economic importance of Picardy?', asked Dr Eugène Lomier in a booklet published in 1936. He was referring to World War I; however, there was to be another war in which the enemy would again take an active interest in the region.

At the start of World War I, Dr Lomier pointed out, the Germans had declared their intention of reaching the Somme. 'La Somme est la voie la plus courte entre la Manche et le Rhin' - 'The Somme is the most direct route between the Channel and the Rhine'. Some 16 years earlier, Dr Lomier's comments had been anticipated in the eloquent opening paragraphs of a booklet by M.G. Garry, Président of the Abbeville Chamber of Commerce. M. Garry similarly pointed out that the natural advantages of the region, enhanced by the Somme canal which linked the port of St Valery to the French canal network, had been recognised by 'notre implacable ennemi, l'Allemand', and by the British to whom the canal was of the greatest importance for provisioning their armies.

The problem lay with the silting of the Bay. Against this, M. Garry proposed either effectively extending the canal into the Bay by means of submerged barriers (a solution which has been at least partly implemented), *or* actually extending the canal, towards Le Hourdel but then inland to Ault and Onival where a deep water port could be created.

Messrs Garry and Lomier were not alone in wishing that the momentum brought by World War I to the port of St Valery might be continued. Proposals for improving ship/rail access at St Valery date from late 1918, and include a suggestion for a metre gauge siding from the approach to St Valery Canal to run alongside the canal, to a berth which could be used by coal ships which tended to be shallow in draught and capable of passing through the lock. This proposal was illustrated in a plan appended to M. Garry's booklet. In May 1919, 14,000 tons of coal were unloaded at St Valery, more than in a whole year before the war. Two-thirds of it went into the CF du Nord's standard gauge wagons.

The standard gauge locomotive rented to the British remained at St Valery, rented now to the SE, until at least the end of the 1920s; throughout this period the SE was striving for agreement with the CF du Nord to allow metre gauge track to be reinstated on the quay and to effect improvements in the track layout. Yet despite the several voices calling for development, and despite the efforts of the SE, the port of St Valery was used less and less. In 1927 the total tonnage was 11,635; in 1928 it fell to 7,832. Dr Lomier blamed the CF du Nord for favouring the ports of Boulogne and Le Tréport at the expense of St Valery. Documentary evidence does not indicate that the CF du Nord was hostile to the port of St Valery, but it is hard to avoid the conclusion that they could have done more to co-operate with the SE in stimulating its use.

The Réseau de la Somme, however, was not inactive between the wars. In the wake of World War I, during which the fleet of locomotives on the SE's Somme network had been significantly reduced, Haine St Pierre in Belgium received an

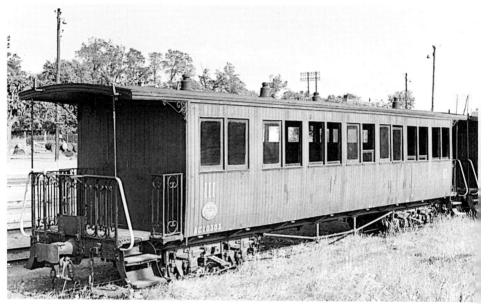

Coach No. AC 10303, built by Manage in 1921, photographed at Noyelles in 1955.
M. Rifault, Collection J-L Rochaix/reproduced with the permission of BVA

One of the Manage coaches, dating from 1921 and restored by the CFBS.   *Ian Tate*

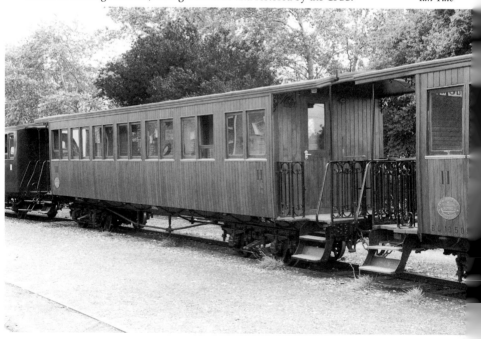

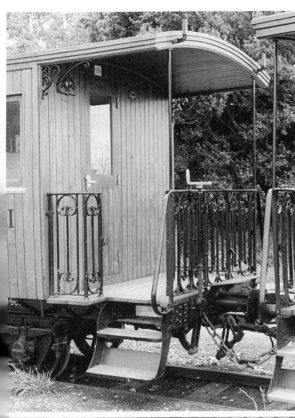

Left: Balcony end of a Manage coach dating from 1921. *Ian Tate*

Below: Interior of one of the Manage coaches. *Ian Tate*

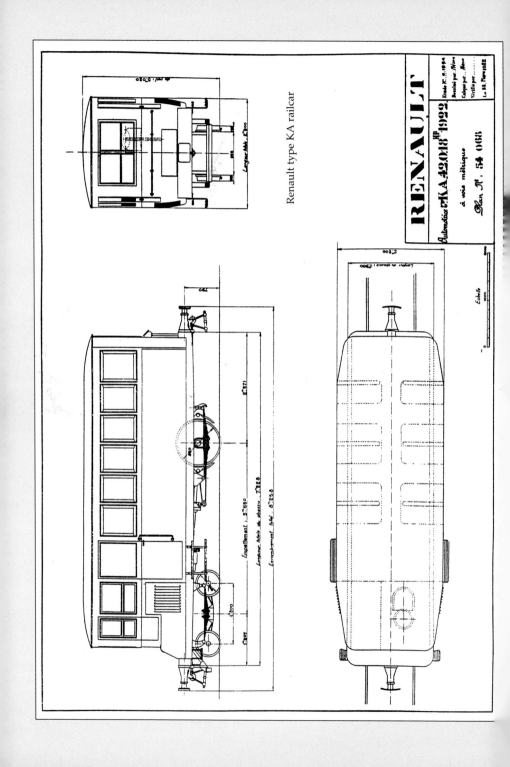

Renault type KA railcar

order for a number of replacement locomotives; these were delivered between May and December 1921. Of these, Nos. 3.851, 3.853, 3.855, 3.856 and 3.615 are known from photographic evidence to have worked on the Réseau des Bains de Mer, although only 3.851 and 3.615 are recorded by Guy Pérève as having been based at St Valery. In 1919 18 passenger carriages were ordered by the SE 'to replace material lost during the war'. These comprised 10 carriages of type Bcf (Nos. 10.501-10.510) providing 2nd and 3rd class accommodation, and eight of type Acf (Nos. 10.301-10.308), 1st and 3rd class. They entered service in 1921.

On 8th December, 1924, the Prefect of the Somme was advised by a memo from the Department's 'Ingénieur en chef des Ponts et Chaussées' that the SE proposed to put into service, on 'certain lines' of the Réseau de la Somme one of two railcars, the purchase of which had been decided by the Conseil Général at its meeting on 24th April, 1923. Two type KA railcars from Renault (*opposite*), and two *remorques* (trailing cars) from Carel et Fouché, had been ordered towards the end of 1923; on 20th May the assistant director of the SE, among others, had visited the Renault factory to inspect the vehicles prior to delivery, and, although broadly satisfied, had insisted that certain accessories be incorporated. The date of delivery is not known; a curiously long time elapsed before the two railcars entered service, one on 6th January, 1925, on the Albert network, and the other on 1st May, 1925, on the 'Réseau des Bains de Mer'.

It is clear that the acquisition of these railcars was something of an experiment. Steam locomotives remained very much the principal motive power through the 1920s, and their dominance was not seriously challenged for some years thereafter. In 1930 [or perhaps earlier?] the SE introduced a number of Campagne petrol *draisines* [trollies] for track maintenance work throughout its Somme network. In 1931, the Département showed some interest in the new Michelin rubber-tyred railcars; the Ingénieur des Ponts et Chaussées briefed the Prefect on this subject in a letter of 27th October, acknowledging that the Michelin vehicles appeared to offer a real step forward in terms of both speed and comfort, but pointing out that they had as yet only been tried on standard gauge lines and recommending waiting until they had proved themselves elsewhere. Some two years later, in 1933, we find the Ingénieur pinpointing three reasons for public discontent with Departmental railways: the poor quality of the track, slowness of trains, and inadequacies in the postal services which they provided. He proposed the replacement of some trains with buses, and use of more powerful railcars on those lines where the track was good enough to permit higher speeds. The two railcars on the Réseau de la Somme were not powerful enough to serve the needs of the service; purchasing cheaper railcars with weak engines was a false economy - it was essential to achieve a faster service - 'une vitesse commerciale notablement plus élevée'. He recommended purchasing three new railcars for the Albert network - a proposal which was turned down by the Conseil Général.

But interest in railcars was not extinguished, and in 1935 the Département sought information from other Departéments concerning their experiences with railcars. A report received from the Département de l'Aisne et d'Allier estimated comparative running costs (F/km) as follows:

Campagne *draisine* dating from 1930 and now preserved by the CFBS.   *Philip Pacey*

De Dion railcar M2 at Le Crotoy. August 1955.   *C.H.A. Townley*

Gauge	1m	1m 44
Steam	3.60	5.00
Railcar (petrol)	2.45	3.15
Railcar (diesel)	2.00	2.35

The Ingénieur en Chef des Ponts et Chaussées who wrote this report favoured using diesel railcars, although he acknowledged that they were not always reliable; in particular, the transmission, 'conceived by constructors as if for cars', often let them down. Also, experience demonstrated that they were better suited to some lines than to others. Another report, from the Département du Cher, gave comparative speeds as follows: steam 25km/h, railcar 40km/h.

The Département d'Indre et Loire reported that railcars which had entered service on 2nd March, 1935, had been well received by the travelling public because of their speed and comfort, and because more frequent services were provided; their introduction had halted the tendency for people to stop travelling by train.

In April 1935 several members of the Conseil Générale accepted an invitation from the SE to experience the performance of railcars in both the Cher and the Allier, on the 11th and 12th April respectively. At its meeting on the 13th and 14th May, the Conseil Général decided on the purchase of 10 railcars. Thirteen manufacturers were contacted; nine responded with proposals; three were shortlisted, and De Dion Bouton was chosen on 20th August. The 10 type NJ 4-wheel railcars (SE Nos. M1-M10) were delivered in February, March, and April, 1936; of these, three were delivered in April to the Réseau des Bains de Mer. Two more De Dion railcars were subsequently acquired in October 1937, and a De Dion railcar and a type NO trailing car (*remorque*) were acquired from the Réseau de la Nièvre in 1939; three other *remorques* seem also to have been acquired from the same source, the four of them being numbered R1-R4, but none of these was destined for St Valery. The depots at St Valery, Albert and St Roch were extended to accommodate the railcars. A De Dion Bouton type NR railcar with bogies, trialled on the Réseau Breton from 1936, rebuilt, and trialled again, was transferred to St Valery in March 1940 where it became No. M21. (It was destroyed by fire at Cayeux in 1958.)

That the SE looked to the introduction of railcars to usher in a new era is demonstrated by a remarkable memorandum circulated to staff of the Réseau de la Somme on 22nd February, 1936. The memo is headed 'Importance de la mise en service des automotrices. Attitude envers le public - Tenue - Propreté du matériel', and it begins thus [my translation]:

The importance of the introduction of railcar services.
Attitude towards the public - Behaviour - Cleanliness of material

The introduction of modern autorails must, like buses, considerably improve the experience of passengers, as much in terms of comfort as in faster journey times, and will accordingly win customers back to the railway. To help us achieve this aim, it is of the first importance to make the best possible impression on the travelling public.

The memo then goes on to list a series of recommendations and guidelines; staff must be polite and smartly turned out; staff must wear the uniforms issued

De Dion railcar M2 and trailing car R4 at Cayeux, August 1956.
B. Rozé, reproduced with the permission of BVA

De Dion railcar M10 at St Valery Canal in 1955.
M. Rifault/Collection J-L Rochaix, reproduced with the permission of BVA

to them; drivers will be issued with overalls and a supply of clean rags so that they can take care of cleaning and greasing vehicles without getting their uniforms dirty; they must keep their faces clean, have regular haircuts, and be correctly 'colleté et cravaté'. Station staff should be dressed in dark blue, men in regulation caps and women wearing armbands. The interior of vehicles should be attended to between journeys; cushions plumped, windows wiped at least once a day. The exterior should be cleaned as often as necessary with water and chamois leather, taking care not to damage the paintwork, in order to 'conserver son aspect brilliant'. Stations must also be kept spick and span. Staff who reside in station buildings were reminded that permission was needed to erect edifices for their personal use, such as hen houses, rabbit hutches, and garden sheds; permission would only be given if the structures were well planned and hidden by foliage so that they did not 'nuire au bon aspect de la gare' ('spoil the appearance of the station'). Drivers, who were also responsible for selling tickets, must be polite and particularly considerate towards the aged and infirm, but should 'avoid all useless conversation' which could cause delays; they should announce stations prior to arrival. Also in order to avoid hold-ups, station staff must, though ever so politely, encourage passengers to get on and off trains without delay. And so on . . .

Of course, modernisation went hand-in-hand with economies; railcars were not only cleaner and more comfortable, but were considerably cheaper to run. In the mid-1920s the SE had come under pressure both from customers and from its own employees: the former, including local business interests, complained that fares and charges were too high; the latter claimed with some justification that they were paid too little for long hours. On 14th January, 1922, Monsieur Th. Gerard of Cayeux wrote to the Prefect asking him to persuade the SE to lower its charges for transporting *galets* and sand from Cayeux to St Valery; a rate of 81 francs 80 per 20 ton wagon in May 1920 had been increased to 159 francs 35! The railway workers wrote to the Prefect to complain that they were expected to work a 9-10 hour day, sometimes starting at 5.00 am and sometimes finishing at 9.30 pm, with only two rest days per month despite the fact that by law they were entitled to 52 rest days per year. So far as wages are concerned, a driver employed by the SE in 1933 could expect a basic annual salary of between 10,000 and 13,000 francs, although various allowances and bonuses might add substantially to this.

It was in this context, then, that the SE sought ways of reducing costs. They drew attention to the requirement laid on them to operate uneconomic services, such as early morning trains which operated largely if not entirely for the benefit of postal traffic; an undated memorandum from this period lists various trains on the Somme network, including train 215, the 6.48 am (5.59 in summer) from Noyelles to St Valery and Cayeux, which 'often run empty'. In 1928 the SE looked to reduce operating costs by modifying the status of various *haltes à faible trafic*, including those at Morlay and St Valery, the recorded (presumably annual) figures for which, at November 1927, were:

	Passengers	Baggage and dogs
St Valery (halt)	8,438	506
Morlay	3,637	162

Track plan of Noyelles station, 1930s.

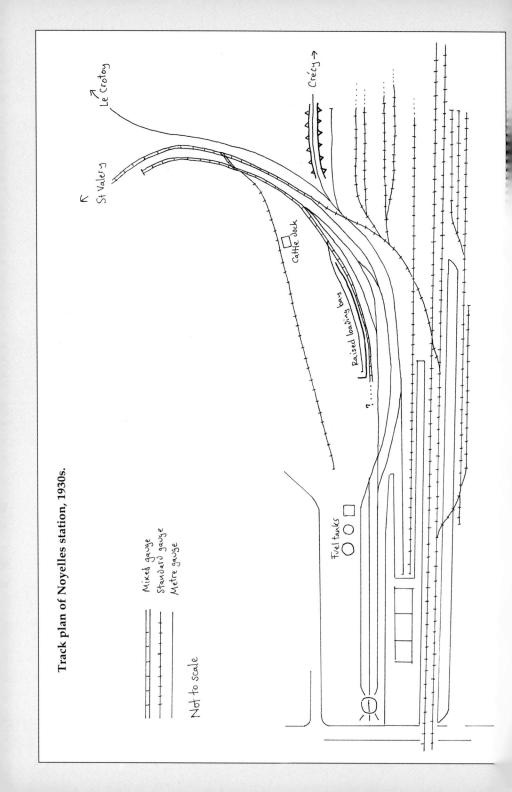

Mixed gauge
Standard gauge
Metre gauge

Not to scale

Le Crotoy →

St Valery

Crécy →

Cattle dock

Raised loading bay

Fuel tanks

Further modifications to station hours were implemented across the Somme network in 1937, partly in connection with the implementation of the 40 hour week; on the 'Réseau des Bains de Mer', Lanchères station building was to be open less often, remaining closed even during the passage of certain trains (the first and last of the day).

Yet even against this background of economies, and as if in response to Dr Lomier's pleas, the SE invested significantly in the 'Réseau des Bains de Mer' towards the end of the 1930s. A halt was established at Pendé-Routhiauville, as from 1st September, 1935. In 1937 a splendid new station was built at St Valery Ville, on the site of the halt nearer to the town, effectively replacing the station at St Valery Canal, the principal building of which was now demolished. Although St Valery Canal was now relegated to the status of a halt, and lost its two raised platforms, it was provided with new, if smaller, buildings - the surviving brick-built single-storey building, incorporating men's and women's toilets, dates from 1937; it carries lettering in the same 1930s style as the station at St Valery Ville, while the hoods over the windows are identical with that on the goods shed at Lanchères, built in 1938. The wooden passenger shelter at St Valery Canal seems likely to have been erected at the same time. The St Valery Ville station is the building which houses the CFBS offices today; its style, sometimes referred to as 'type Deauville', distinguishes it from the other stations and is characteristic of its decade. This was part of a grandiose plan of reconstruction which would also have resulted in a new station at Cayeux had World War II not intervened. (Alternative designs for the *agrandissement* of Cayeux station, drawn up in 1930 and 1931, are reproduced in *Cayeux d'hier*.)

St Valery Ville station seen from the west.   *Philip Pacey*

Lanchères acquired a new goods shed in 1938, and the crossing keeper's cottage at Hurt was doubled in size in 1939.

Timetables from the 1930s show that the basic winter services generally comprised five or six trains each way between Noyelles and Le Crotoy, and between Noyelles and Cayeux, with perhaps two or three additional 'shuttle' trains between Noyelles and St Valery, operated by a mix of railcars and locomotive-hauled trains. Also working in and out of Noyelles were two steam-hauled trains and a railcar service to Forest l'Abbaye. Additional trains might be scheduled for weekends or holidays, and were included in summer timetables, making a total of between 8 and 10 services in each direction between Noyelles and Le Crotoy and Noyelles and Cayeux. More or less simultaneous arrivals and departures of two or even three metre gauge trains at Noyelles, in order to connect with main line trains to and from Amiens and Paris, were as ever a feature of the timetable. Concerns of local people, and the role of the Prefect, are illustrated by a dossier in the Archives at Amiens dating from 1935. The Conseil Municipal of Le Crotoy wrote to the Prefect to protest against the SE's 'suppression' of train No. 6, the 10.34 departure from Le Crotoy. Their argument is that this will oblige northbound travellers to leave on the 9.20 (No. 4) and then wait two hours at Noyelles; they suggest cancellation instead of train No. 4. The Prefect, on checking with the SE and taking advice from staff within the Département, points out that No. 4 provides a perfectly good connection for the north, since a train bound for Boulogne leaves Noyelles at 9.44, and he questions the community's wisdom in apparently being more anxious about northbound than southbound connections: 'Has there been a shift in the orientation of the interests of the people of Le Crotoy? It isn't likely'.

The SE's endeavours to modernise the railway in the late 1930s may have been astutely judged. In 1938 the French Government decided that public transport should be better co-ordinated. The main line railway companies were amalgamated, bringing into being the SNCF. So far as regional and local transport was concerned, each Département was obliged to submit a *plan de transport*, eliminating any wasteful competition between different forms of transport. Where a light railway and a bus service had operated over similar routes, one, usually the railway, was compulsorily closed. Over a third of the total mileage of local railways was lost, including not just struggling concerns but also some efficient, well-run lines.

Chapter Six

The 'Réseau des Bains de Mer' during World War II

On 21st May, 1940 German troops, preceded by fleeing French and Belgian refugees, reached the Baie de Somme. They remained for four years. Although it is known that trains on the 'Réseau des Bains de Mer' - the metre gauge lines which linked the seaside towns of Le Crotoy, St Valery, and Cayeux, to the main line at Noyelles - continued to operate, and that the line was utilised by the Germans, the story of the railway during World War II remains largely untold and little investigated. If for entirely understandable reasons, it seems that local people do not wish to recall or be reminded of this time. Yet one notable piece of evidence survives in part: the 'graveyard' of locomotives beside the line just outside St Valery. And a remarkable exception to the apparent lack of written memoirs is provided by Count Joseph de Valicourt, whose book *La Baie de Somme* includes a blow-by-blow account of the course of events as experienced by an inhabitant of Noyelles.

Noyelles, being on the main line, saw, and suffered from, a good deal of unwelcome activity. German troops installed themselves as uninvited guests in Noyelles homes from 22nd May, 1940, one of their principal tasks being to guard the station. On 24th December there was a flurry of activity at the station; it was said afterwards that Hitler had passed through on his way to inspect troops at Laviers. On 24th October, 1941 a train which was stopped in the station was attacked from the air and the locomotive was 'literally cut in two'. The station was strafed by Allied aircraft on several occasions during the war; on 28th April, 1942 three railway employees were hit and one was killed. On 22nd June, 1942 the Germans installed an anti-aircraft battery, hidden among the dikes, close to the Noyelles-St Valery railway line. On 31st July, Belgian conscripts began building ramps at Noyelles station to facilitate the unloading of tanks. In November (sometime between the 17th and the 22nd) the 'little train' (Noyelles-St Valery) was hit (at Noyelles?) and several railway workers were wounded. On 29th November a British plane, strafing a main-line train, hit overhead wires and crashed. On 2nd December, St Valery station was attacked from the air and the water tower was destroyed, inconveniencing the Germans who, De Valicourt tells us, used this railway often.

An intensification of activities in 1942 followed a relatively tranquil period which had started in June 1941. Prior to June 1941 the Germans had been planning to invade England; from 1942, they feared invasion from England.

The Atlantic Wall

In order to appreciate why the Baie de Somme, and the area around Cayeux in particular, became a scene of especially intense activity from the autumn of 1942, it may be helpful to look back and to examine in more detail than hitherto the history of the *exploitation des galets*. From around the mid-19th century, the gathering and crushing of flint pebbles (*galets*) flourished around Cayeux, where such pebbles exist in profusion beneath the sand dunes and piled high by the tides along the sea-front. Since 1886, the year of the opening of the railway from St Valery to Cayeux, the former practice of transporting pebbles by barge, from Cayeux round the point of Le Hourdel and into the bay to St Valery, came to an end; Decauville-type track of 600 mm gauge was used to enable trucks of pebbles to be brought from the beach and various excavations to the station at Cayeux. In the town of Cayeux, one 600 mm route was laid along the rue Dumont d'Urville, the rue l'Ecce Homo, and the rue du Chevalier de la Barre, while another followed the length of the chemin des Biais. Sections of these lines can be seen in numerous old photographs and picture postcards (*see pages 51 & 52*); today, rusty lengths of rail can be found re-used as fence posts in and around Cayeux, and the remains of at least one section of Decauville track lies half buried in sand on the beach at low tide. There was also a 600 mm network from an extraction site onto a projecting jetty in the harbour at Le Hourdel; one photograph shows a *steam* locomotive working on this jetty *(see page 53)*; at least part of this system remained in use for a decade or more after the war*. To the south of Cayeux, *exploitation des galets* was initiated at Hautebut by a Belgian, Anselme Daive, from 1910. Daive established his headquarters at 11, rue de la Ferté, St Valery. Pebbles were moved from coastal excavations at Hautebut to a point closer to the road utilising skip wagons on 600 mm track, but were then transported by 9 ton lorries along the road to Lanchères, where they were transferred to trains.

Thus, the Cayeux area presented the occupying Germans with a natural resource for constructing coastal defences, in exactly the right place, and with an active industry for exploiting it; at the same time, intensive extraction of material from the area immediately behind the coastline would itself make the terrain less accommodating to invading forces. The task of constructing these defences was entrusted to the Organisation Todt (OT). The OT had come into being in 1933 to build *autobahns* in Germany; it was named after Dr Fritz Todt, builder of the Siegfried Line, who was appointed Inspector General of German Road Construction in 1933. Todt died in 1942, and was succeeded by Albert Speer. In occupied territory the OT commandeered local construction companies and made use of conscripted labour. The Service Obligatoire du Travail (STO), introduced in 1942, involved forced labour including the removal of workers to Germany. The OT paid better wages than French companies, but in any case was able to attract volunteers who hoped that working for the OT in France would save them from being sent to work in Germany (a vain hope, in some cases).

Joseph de Valicourt records that in Noyelles, the first signs of the building of coastal defences were seen in September and October, 1942, with the arrival of one contingent after another of troops and engineers; the newly arrived personnel were, as ever, billeted in local homes. On the 28th October some junior officers arrived who 'drew up plans for fortifications in my garden'. On 11th November a blockhouse was built in a nearby field. More Germans arrived in April 1943. From November, says De Valicourt, life became almost

---

* In an obituary of his father, CFBS member Charles-Edouard Girode recalled a failed attempt at visiting the Chatelet works at Le Hourdel in the 1960s or thereabouts, where there was a 600 mm tramway complete with locotractors (*Ch'tchot Train* No. 24 June, 1996 p. 12).

unbearable, due to the incessant passage of new troops sent to fortify or guard the region, the construction of shelters, trenches, and *hérissons*, the aerial attacks which all this activity attracted, and anxiety among the German ranks. On the 12th November more men arrived, to mark out sites and clear trees and hedges. On 21st November it was made known that some 3,000 Organisation Todt personnel would be arriving shortly. On 22nd November it was announced that local men of up to 45 years of age would be required to help build defences. December saw the construction of V1 rocket launch ramps, at inland sites (such as Crécy) well out of the range of the guns of ships in the Channel.

At Cayeux, it was said, 'on coule du béton partout' - that is to say, 'Concrete flows everywhere'. Today, it is possible to see whole pebbles mixed into the concrete of surviving German blockhouses, especially where the surface is cracked or broken. Was it the case that crushed pebbles were also part of the mixture? As soon as he took command of the 'B' armies (responsible for the entire zone between the rivers Escaut and Loire*) at the beginning of 1944, Rommel brought a new momentum to the building of the Atlantic Wall. He visited Cayeux five times to inspect progress, and he insisted on the necessity of setting up an exceptionally dense barrier of obstacles to obstruct landing craft, tanks, and infantry. An anti-tank wall was built along the top of the beach. Obstacles placed on the beaches here included *asperges Rommel* - 'Rommel's asparagus' (*see below*), *tétraèdres en béton* (*see below*), and *hérissons tchèques* - 'Czech hedgehogs', constructed of metal but often set in a concrete base.

De Valicourt records 23rd January as the date of Rommel's first visit to the area. It was after this, on 10th February, that civil engineers began to flood the low-lying land near Noyelles. The river Dien was blocked where the railway to St Valery crossed it, and elsewhere; its rising waters overflowed onto the road to St Valery on 24th February.

On the 7th April single women at St Valery were requisitioned to place *asperges Rommel* in the fields. De Valicourt describes these as 'young trees of 15-20 cms diameter, 4-5 metres high, intended to prevent gliders from landing. Mines were placed at the top of some of these, and were linked to mines on some of the others'. On 27th April single women aged between 18 and 45 were similarly requisitioned at Noyelles. On 16th April holes were prepared for mines in the railway bridge supporting the St Valery line (presumably the bridge over the river Dien) at Noyelles.

On 13th May, 1944, during his third visit, Rommel expressed dissatisfaction regarding the production of *tétraèdres*, which consisted of six pieces of concrete 1.50 cm in length which were assembled together *in situ*. But he was pleased with the 230,000 concrete posts (*pieux*) which had been put in place. These posts were known simply as 'Rommels'. Rommel also ordered the flooding of the 'Bas-Champs' behind Cayeux.

---

* The 348 Infanterie Division, under Generalleutnant Paul Seyffart, was responsible for the sector between the Baie de Somme and Le Tréport; their headquarters was at Friville. The 344 ID was responsible for the area from the Baie de Somme northwards to Stella Plage.

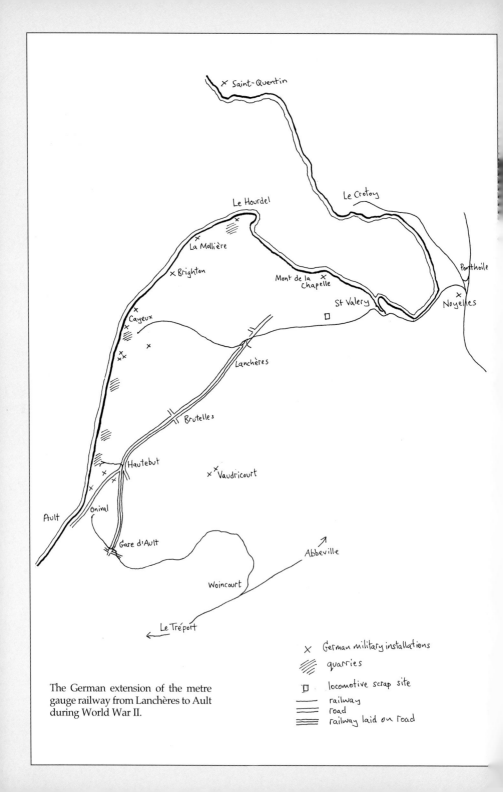

× Saint-Quentin

Le Crotoy

Le Hourdel

La Mollière

× Brighton

Mont de la
Chapelle

St Valery

Porthoïle

Noyelles

Cayeux

×

× ×

Lanchères

Brutelles

Hautebut

× Vaudricourt

Ault

Onival

Gare d'Ault

Abbeville

Woincourt

Le Tréport

× German military installations

quarries

▢ locomotive scrap site

── railway

═ road

═ railway laid on road

The German extension of the metre
gauge railway from Lanchères to Ault
during World War II.

The Railway

What of the railway? In Cayeux, the Organisation Todt augmented the existing Decauville tramways by putting down temporary 600 mm rails from the beach to the station along the avenue Paul Doumer, through the centre of the town - the most direct route possible. This was possibly less for removing pebbles from the beaches than for carrying materials to it. But, much more ambitiously, they laid a metre-gauge line along the road from the metre gauge railway at Lanchères towards Ault - the same route used by the Daive company's lorries. Robert Salmon has written that this metre gauge line terminated at Hautebut, where there was extensive quarrying, and that a 600 mm gauge line was laid from Hautebut along the road to Ault station on the standard gauge Woincourt-Onival branch line, thus providing two routes for transporting material from the Hautebut site. However, the evidence of aerial photographs, while not definitive, appears to show the metre gauge track continuing across the road junction in the village of Hautebut and being joined at this point by a branch line from the quarries (*see page 88*). In a particularly revealing sequence of photographs shot from a sortie on 3rd March, 1944, a train with locomotives at front and rear, both locomotives emitting plumes of smoke, can be seen proceeding southwards from Hautebut - locomotives travelling in this direction would have to work hard, since the road is climbing above the *falaise mort*. The line continued along this road (the D940) to join the standard gauge line at Ault station. Aerial photographs do not disclose exactly what happened at the junction of metre and standard gauge tracks, although the metre gauge line appears to curve off the road in the direction of Onival. What is certain is that the Germans did make considerable use of the standard gauge branch from Woincourt, on which passenger trains had ceased to run in May 1939, for moving materials for the Atlantic Wall; they employed SNCF 0-8-0 tank locomotives and their crews (including two from the depot at Le Tréport and one from Abbeville; one of these was No. 4.313) as well as the resident 2-4-0 tank locomotives, and the track suffered under heavier loads; both Allied aircraft and Resistance fighters thought it worth targetting the line. On one occasion (in 1944) sabotage by the Resistance caused a train to derail and topple off an embankment near Friville. It seems that the Germans had no use for the station buildings at Onival, which they blew up on 17th July, 1943. (It may be that they were in the line of sight of a gun emplacement.)

Elsewhere on the 'Réseau des Bains de Mer' aerial photographs reveal a mystery. It appears that a link was made between the Le Crotoy line and the main line at Ponthoile; there can be no other explanation for a graceful curve cut through the fields between the lines, which is visible on photographs in March 1944 but of which there is no sign in photographs taken two years earlier. It - whatever it was - surely has to have been the work of the Organisation Todt? But what exactly was its purpose? (*See page 89*.)

The German occupation forces would have found several metre gauge locomotives at their disposal hereabouts; those of the SE, responsible for operation of the Réseau des Bains de Mer, as well as (probably) the Orenstein & Koppel locomotive belonging to the sugar-beet factory at Lanchères. But it

Aerial view of Hautebut, as seen from an Allied aircraft on the morning of 3rd March, 1944. The village of Hautebut is in the lower centre; a row of trees marks the road to Lanchères, on which temporary metre gauge track was laid. Two plumes of smoke, assumed to be from steam locomotives, can be seen at the bottom of the picture (*left of centre*) on the road towards Ault station. Track is surely also present on the unmetalled road leading from Hautebut towards the quarry on the coast (*upper left*); indeed, the gentle curve out of the village has the appearance of having been cut out specifically to accommodate rail traffic and to avoid the sharp corner on the road to its right.

Air Photo Library, University of Keele, reproduced with permission from the Ministry of Defence

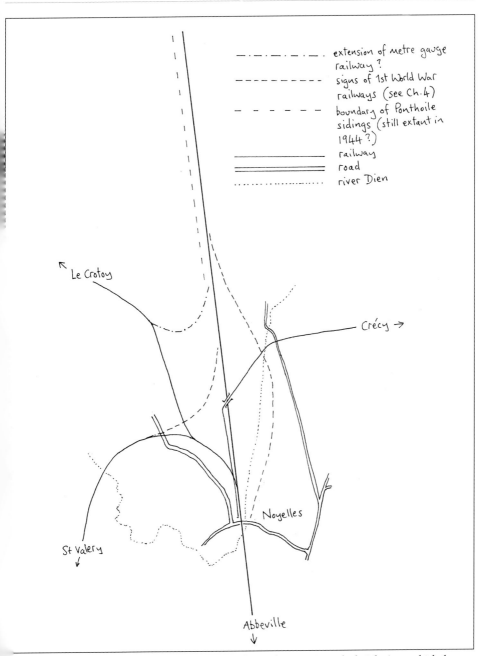

Tracing from an aerial photograph of Noyelles, 7th March, 1944. From the height from which the photograph was taken, actual rails cannot be discerned. However, the photograph appears to show a new link from the Le Crotoy line to sidings beside the main line at Ponthoile.

Above, left: Locomotives in the scrap dump near St Valery, photographed in 1952. *From the left:* Corpet Louvet 0-6-2T No. 534 *Suzanne,* Corpet Louvet 0-6-0T No. 1104, Corpet Louvet 0-6-0T No. 927, and a Pinguely 0-6-0T. *P. Laurent/Collection K. Clingan. Above, right:* Corpet Louvet 0-6-2T No. 534 *Suzanne* in the scrap dump at St Valery, photographed in 1954, and still complete with side tanks, name plate, and maker's plate. *P. Laurent. Bottom, left:* Deterioration takes its toll. Corpet Louvet 0-6-2T No. 534 *Suzanne* in the scrap dump at St Valery. By this time it had lost its side tanks. *G. Pérève. Bottom, right:* Rescue! Corpet Louvet 0-6-2T No. 534 *Suzanne* being removed from the scrap dump at St Valery on 24th April, 1981. *G. Pérève*

seems that these were not enough, and that at least nine more locomotives were brought from elsewhere. After the war, nine locomotives were left behind in a scrap dump belonging to a M. Vaillant, next to the line just outside St Valery. Four remain, one having been removed as recently as 1996; they are of course in a very poor state. The nine locomotives were as follows:

0-6-2T Corpet No. 534 of 1890. Originally from the Compagnie Meusienne de Chemins de Fer where it was No. 26 and called *Suzanne*, this locomotive subsequently worked for the Grands Travaux de France. After nearly 40 years at St Valery, it was purchased and removed in 1981 by the Syndicat d'Initiative de Bar-le-Duc and is being restored.

0-6-0T Corpet-Louvet No. 1104 of 1904. Originally from the Lunéville-Einville railway, this locomotive subsequently worked for the Sablières de la Haute et Basse Seine. This locomotive remains at St Valery.

0-6-0T Corpet-Louvet No. 927 of 1903, from the Economique des Charentes where it carried the number 47. This locomotive is still at St Valery.

0-6-0T Pinguely. This locomotive was acquired and removed from the scrap heap by the Association des Amis du Petit Anjou in 1996, the intention being to restore it as a static exhibit. Following close examination, the identity of this locomotive is now being questioned. Previously thought to have been Pinguely No. 116 of 1901, delivered to the Tramway de l'Indre, it is now suspected of being one of a series, Nos. 70-76, 79 and 80, ordered in 1899 for the Compagnie des Chemins de fer du Beaujolais.

0-6-2T Schneider of 1891, one of the series 2456-2467 delivered to the Département de la Côte d'Or. This locomotive is still at St Valery.

0-6-0T Pinguely. Details not known. This locomotive is still at St Valery.

0-6-0T, unidentified, scrapped in the 1950s.

0-6-0T of German origin, scrapped.

0-4-0T Corpet-Louvet, unidentified, but with Brown valve gear. Acquired and removed in 1989 by a member of the Musée des Transports de la Vallée du Sausseron, Valmondois.

Assuming that all of these locomotives were used by the Germans here, then the number of locomotives as well as the laying of additional track is a measure

The scrap dump at St Valery seen in August 1955.   *C.H.A. Townley*

One of the two entrances to the air raid shelter at St Valery Canal. *Philip Pacey*

of a considerable level of activity. Are we to suppose that, in addition to providing materials for the defences on its own length of coast, this area was a source of supplies - of flint pebbles (whole or crushed), of concrete components, and perhaps of sand, to other sectors, with material being trans-shipped onto standard gauge trains at Noyelles and at Ault? It is said that transhipment of materials from metre gauge to standard gauge took place at St Valery Canal. As well as or instead of Noyelles? Was St Valery, being away from the main line, felt to be less vulnerable to attack from the air?

Some local people were obliged to work for the Organisation Todt through the STO; if some of these 'volunteered' it would have been in the hope of not being sent to work in Germany. One worker, M. Testu (the father of Maurice Testu of the CFBS), remembers having taken part in the 'déchargements successifs des locomotives, des sacs de ciment, et des bétonneuses' - that is, the unloading of locomotives(!), of sacks of cement, and of cement mixers - at St Valery Canal. While he was unloading cement, British aircraft attacked and he took shelter under the loaded wagons, happy in the knowledge that the sacks of cement provided added protection. A concrete air raid shelter, with two entrances above curved stairways leading to a sunken corridor, survives to this day at St Valery Canal. At Cayeux, M. Sifflet, a locomotive driver, was killed by machine gun fire during an Allied air raid.

The very intensity of German activities attracted the attention of Allied aircraft: the railway, the construction sites, and the factory for crushing pebbles at Le Hourdel, were all targets. On 4th May, 1944, the railway depot at St Valery was destroyed by fire, presumably as a result of a bombing raid; two railcars and one locomotive, which were inside the depot, were also destroyed. During this or another raid the road bridge over the canal to St Valery Canal station was destroyed. Henceforth the road was re-routed over the hitherto rail-only swing bridge: this bridge was to be dynamited by the retreating Germans in September, effectively blocking canal, road and rail.

The summer 1942 *Indicateur Chaix, Région Nord* shows (in table 297) a decimated passenger service in operation, with just three trains in each direction between Noyelles, St Valery, and Cayeux, and three between Noyelles and Le Crotoy. Trains are scheduled to arrive at Noyelles at 7.52 and 7.55, 12.00 and 12.11, and 14.30 and 14.52, and to depart at 8.35 and 8.45, and subsequently (note the pattern of near simultaneous departures) at 12.45 and 12.46, and at 20.41 and 20.42. Four services are provided by autorail: the 8.35 from Noyelles to Le Crotoy, the 12.00 from Le Crotoy to Noyelles (arriving at Noyelles at 12.11), the 12.45 from Noyelles to St Valery and Cayeux, and the return service from Cayeux, departing at 14.20. This means that there would have had to have been two locomotives in steam from quite early in the morning - to haul the 7.08 from Cayeux and the 7.36 from Le Crotoy - but that subsequently these locomotives and their crews would have hardly been overstretched by the scant requirements of the passenger timetable. Further, there was a six hour gap between the arrival of trains at 14.30 and 14.52 at Noyelles, and the 20.41 and 20.42 departures, the last passenger trains of the day. The January 1944 *Indicateur Chaix, Région Nord* shows a very similar timetable, again with just three trains in each direction on each line. In this case there is no sign that autorails were used for any of the services. Again, there is a noticeable lack of passenger trains, from the 14.12 and 14.16 arrivals at Noyelles until the final departures from Noyelles at 20.50 and 20.52 (an hour earlier on Sundays and holidays). No doubt this long spell every day without passenger trains facilitated use of the railway for other purposes.

The end of the War and its aftermath

Bombs which fell near St Valery on the night of 2nd June, 1944 were among those Allied activities intended to keep the Germans guessing as to where the Allies planned to invade. 'So it was with emotion and even disbelief that we learned, at nearly 11 o'clock on 6th June, of the landings on the Calvados Channel coasts' says Joseph de Valicourt. From this moment, signs of German unrest were apparent. On the night of 19th August, the Resistance blew up the water tower at Noyelles station; men were requisitioned to repair the damage the same night. On 1st September an ammunition train in a siding was blown up. On the morning of 2nd September people woke up to the sound of gunfire; English and Polish troops, having reached St Valery, were bombarding the Germans at Le Crotoy and Ponthoile from the 'Colline aux Moineaux'. De Valicourt notes that a shepherd took his sheep out to graze on the salt marshes nonetheless: 'and when asked about this historic day, he simply said 'the animals had to eat, just like any other day!' During the following night the Germans vanished.

What of the war's aftermath, especially so far as the 'Réseau des Bains de Mer' was concerned? The seaside trade, which was the railway's principal *raison d'être*, could not fail to have been badly affected. Le Hourdel had been razed to the ground; the tiny resort of Brighton, named after the English town across the Channel, was in ruins; villas and holiday camps had been destroyed. At Cayeux, many villas had been demolished by the Germans, in some cases to make way for, or to avoid blocking the view from, block-houses; one of these survives intact in Cayeux, and the base of at least one other also remains; many more can be seen in varying states of preservation along the coast. It took more than four years to clear mines from the beach, the dunes, and the low-lying land behind the dunes. But the railway went on running, no doubt playing its part in the work of recovery and reconstruction, and continuing to serve the flint, or silica, industry which prospered, and flourishes to this day - though nowadays using lorries while the railway survives as a tourist attraction.

Chapter Seven

The 'Réseau des Bains de Mer' After World War II

On 23rd May, 1945 a young man from St Valery, returning home from an eventful war, descended from a main line train at Noyelles and looked for a metre gauge train to take him to the eagerly anticipated conclusion of his journey. Alas! there was no little train - the staff were on strike. At the end of the war the omens were not good for the 'Réseau des Bains de Mer'. The post-war years saw the closure of many light railways in France. The petrol shortage during the war had brought traffic back to the railways, but in many cases the unforeseen wear and tear, unaccompanied by investment in maintenance or renewal, brought them to breaking point. The 'Réseau des Bains de Mer' had borne more than its share of wear and tear; at the same time, the holiday resorts which it served had suffered gravely. The 1947 Monnet plan briefly held out a promise of government aid for some 3,500 miles of secondary lines which were identified as essential, but nothing came of this so far as the 'Réseau des Bains de Mer' was concerned. And yet the 'Réseau des Bains de Mer' did survive, partly because of its role in serving seaside resorts, but also because it was still of value to local industry. Indeed some argued that, far from being closed, it should be developed, and converted to standard gauge.

The activities of the Germans in this area of Occupied France during the war had provided stimulus to the extraction and construction industries which subsequently had a part to play in the post-war era. Thus it is interesting to note that in August 1946 M. Guicheteau, a sub-director of the SE, wrote to M. Dorizou, director of Cie Centrale des Emeris et Tous Abrasifs, a silica processing works at Le Hourdel, outlining proposals for converting the Baie de Somme railway (including Noyelles-Le Crotoy as well as St Valery-Cayeux) to standard gauge, building an extension to Le Hourdel, and operating the line with diesel-electric railcars and locomotives.* M. Guicheteau's purpose seems to have been to seek participants to form a syndicate to obtain funding of the order of 150-200 million francs - at least 75 million to relay track, at least 20-30 million for three railcars, and at least 50 million for three locomotives. In 1949 this project was still being considered. A typescript, reproduced in *Ch'tchot Train* (No. 33 June 1997), estimated that 57 million francs would be needed for track work and 36 million for two diesel locomotives; it was envisaged that the metre gauge track would be retained in a mixed gauge formation as far as Lanchères, presumably so that the sugar beet refinery could continue to use its metre gauge locomotives and metre gauge wagons. The money, with something to spare, was to be raised by the sale of redundant installations (buildings?

* In fact similar proposals had punctuated the history of the metre gauge line to Cayeux. The idea of converting the line from St Valery to Cayeux to standard gauge was discussed or formally proposed by the people of Cayeux in 1911, 1912, 1916, 1927, 1928, 1944, 1948 and 1949. Lanchères asked for the line from St Valery to be converted to standard gauge in 1963. Proposals for a standard gauge rail link from St Valery to Le Hourdel were made in 1910 and 1933, and for an extension of the metre gauge line from Cayeux to Le Hourdel in 1945 and 1946.

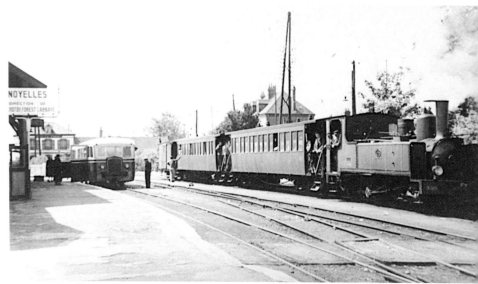

Noyelles: the metre gauge terminus from the north in 1949. The railcar is destined for Le Crotoy; to the right, a train for Cayeux is to be hauled by locomotive No. 3.526.

P. Laurent/Collection K. Clingan

De Dion Bouton railcar X-158 at Noyelles, November 1972.   *Geoffrey Nickson*

land? equipment?) and from compensation for war damage. Perhaps sadly - if not for narrow gauge enthusiasts - nothing was to come of all these plans, though some 20 years later, in his 'Light Railways News' column in the July 1968 issue of *Railway World*, W.J.K. Davies wrote that 'plans are in being for converting the St-Valéry-Cayeux section of the Réseau de la Somme to standard gauge and then closing the shorter branch from Noyelles to Le Crotoy. No date has been fixed'.

The fact that it survived while many other minor railways were closing enabled the 'Réseau des Bains de Mer' to benefit from materials and stock no longer needed elsewhere. Some of the St Valery-Cayeux line was relaid with 25 kg rails recovered from the neighbouring standard gauge Woincourt-Onival line, on which passenger trains ceased in May 1939 and which closed altogether from 1st January, 1947. Interestingly, many of these rails (which remained in use until 1992) bore the stamp of the British War Department; clearly they had been brought to France to be utilised during World War I.

The extraordinary activities of World War II had brought a variety of steam locomotives to the Baie de Somme, and in 1949, following the closure of the Réseau d'Albert (part of the Somme network), some of the SE's Haine St-Pierre 2-6-0Ts were transferred to the 'Réseau des Bains de Mer'. However, this was destined to be a final flourish for steam traction. Even before the war, railcars had become an important element in the operation of the 'Réseau des Bains de Mer'. In the years following the war, more diesel-powered vehicles arrived, in most cases from lines elsewhere which were being closed. A 4-wheel railcar, M-31, constructed by VFIL at its workshops at Lumbres, was acquired new by the SE in 1957. Three bogie railcars, numbered M-41 to M-43, built by VFIL at its workshops at Lumbres in 1936, were transferred from elsewhere: M-41 from the Flandres network line; M-42 and M-43 from the Persan-Beaumont-Hermes line. All three arrived in 1955. Two diesel locomotives, Nos. 351 and 352, built in the VFIL workshops at Lumbres for the Flandres network in 1951, arrived in 1957, (According to one source - *Les Trains oubliées* - it was specifically for the benefit of these locomotives that an intervening wagon fitted with twin and centre various buffers and couplings was introduced between the locomotive and standard gauge wagons.)

A third diesel locomotive, No. 301 (apparently renumbered 353 for a while) was acquired in August 1960. Built by VFIL at Lumbres for the Anvin-Calais line, it had been sold to the Régie Départementales des Transports des Ardennes in 1956. In 1971, two De Dion Bouton type OC1 bogie railcars, Nos. X-157 and X-158, built in 1937 for the Côtes-du-Nord, were transferred from the Réseau Breton. X-158 was subsequently transferred by the Compagnie de Générale Chemins de Fer et de Transports Automobiles (CFTA) to Corsica; however, custody of X-157 would later pass to the CFBS.

Finally, trailing car R-6 was also transferred from the Réseau Breton in 1971. This vehicle, built in 1937, was originally one of seven Billard type 150 railcars on the Tramways Ille & Vilaine which, after being transferred to the Réseau Breton in 1952, suffered the removal of their 150hp engines in the process of being converted to trailing cars or 'remorques'. Three, but not R-6, were subsequently re-fitted with engines.

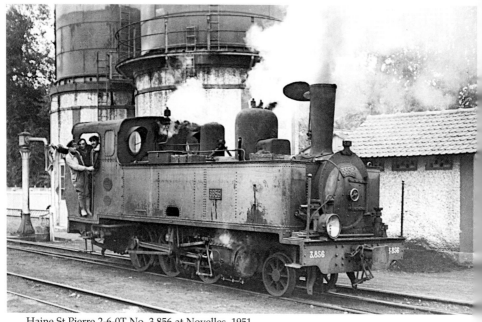

Haine St Pierre 2-6-0T No. 3.856 at Noyelles, 1951.
M. Rifault/Collection J-L Rochaix, reproduced with the permission of BVA

SACM 0-6-2T No. 3.561 at St Valery Canal in 1955.
M. Rifault/Collection: J-L Rochaix, reproduced with the permission of BVA

The October 1947 timetable shows just one morning and one afternoon train daily, in each direction between Le Crotoy and Noyelles and St Valery and Noyelles; in 1947, services still operated on the third metre gauge line out of Noyelles towards Forest l'Abbaye, and, three times during the day there were triple near-simultaneous arrivals or departures at Noyelles, connecting with main line trains: arrivals were scheduled at 6.55, 7.00 and 7.03, and at 15.56, 16.00 and 16.01, and departures at 17.30, 17.32 and 17.33.

Staffing the Railway

How many staff did it take to run the railway? Or to ask the same question in another way, what contribution did the railway make to the local economy as an employer, and how many jobs would be lost if it closed down? Having sifted through salary records for the year 1950, I can offer the following figures for the number of staff employed on the 'Réseau des Bains de Mer':

St Valery	1 chef de gare (Ville)
	1 chef de gare (Canal)
	1 chef de dépôt
	2 chefs d'équipe (platelayers' foremen)
	1 chef de réserve (store-keeper)
	1 inspecteur
	1 surveillant
	1 chef ouvrier (chief mechanic)
	2 chefs de train (passenger train guards)
	1 conducteur autorail (autorail guard)
	2 menuisiers (carpenters)
	1 ajusteur (metalworker)
	1 tourneur (lathe operator)
	4 mécaniciens (drivers)
	5 chauffeurs (firemen) of whom 1 doubled as a platelayer
	8 ouvriers (mechanics)
	2 employées (office workers?)
	12 cantonniers (platelayers)
	1 facteur mixte (porters)
	1 factrice (a female porter)
	2 gardes barrières (crossing keepers)
Cayeux	1 chef de gare
	1 chef de train
	2 facteurs chefs (senior porters)
	2 mécaniciens
	1 chauffeur
Le Crotoy	1 chef de gare
	1 chef de train
	2 facteurs chefs
	1 mécanicien
	1 chauffeur
	1 conducteur autorail

A train at St Valery Canal behind Haine St Pierre 2-6-0T No. 3.853 in 1955.
M. Rifault/Collection J-L Rochaix, reproduced with the permission of BVA

The arrival of a train at Cayeux, behind Ateliers Nord 0-6-2T No. 3.526, sometime in the 1950s.
Collection J-L Rochaix, reproduced with the permission of BVA

Lanchères	1 *chef de gare*
Hurt	1 *garde barrières* (and 1 relief)
Noyelles	1 *garde barrières*
Total	68

Basic salaries mostly varied from around 12,000 to around 19,000 francs per month; the *chef de dépôt* earned some 28,000 francs and the inspector 27,000 francs, while the crossing-keepers, who were presumably employed solely to stand guard when trains passed by, received less than anyone.* It is interesting to note that all staff on the 'Réseau des Bains de Mer' received a monthly *Balnéaire* bonus of 600 francs in each of the holiday months of June, July, August and September. It may seem surprising that no staff were employed at the station at Noyelles; this would have been because operations there were controlled by SNCF staff. (Eight people, including the station master, posed for a photograph of the station staff at Noyelles which illustrated an article in *La Vie du Rail* in 1958.)

In a book published in 1956 an English visitor, Bryan Morgan, noted that 'one branch still uses steam as frequently as little De Dion Boutons, and more frequently when the holiday-makers come flooding up at summer weekends'. In the course of painting a somewhat bleak picture, Morgan wrote of conductors 'abandoning ship in mid-journey, finding a bicycle in the hedgerows and vanishing down a long straight road', and of a guard who used a bicycle to overtake a train 'stolen by a small boy'. (This story - the truth or otherwise of which I have been unable to confirm - is celebrated by a poem in the Picard dialect, reprinted and translated in Appendix Three.) He also noted that departures from Noyelles 'occur within a couple of minutes of each other', and that 'arrivals are all-but simultaneous, too; and in fact I suspect some genuine racing after the last halts on each line, in order to get precedence into the main line junction of Noyelles'.

Other English visitors in the 1950s included Peter Allen and P.B. Whitehouse; although the Baie de Somme does not feature prominently in their classic book *Narrow Gauge Railways of Europe*, it is the first railway they visit and as such is vividly evoked in their preface: 'The evening railcar from Cayeux-sur-Mer to St-Valéry-sur-Somme and Noyelles ran 10 minutes late and nearly hit a cow, all because of delay on the Southern Region of British Railways'. Connections with main line trains at Noyelles were maintained at all costs, causing one metre gauge train to wait and later ones to hurry. Yet another English enthusiast, D. Trevor Rowe, visited the line in 1955, but his account of his trip was not published until 1961, when it was revised by W.J.K. Davies who had visited the line in 1960. In 1955 Trevor Rowe was much taken with the scene at St Valery Ville, where (forming his first impressions through English eyes, before grasping the character and extent of St Valery) he describes 'a very small station right in front of the village green':

---

* 1950 was the year in which France introduced a minimum wage, originally known as the *smig* (salaire minimal national interprofessionnel garanti) and set at 78 francs per hour. For someone paid at this level, a 40 hour week would therefore yield 3,120 francs, and a monthly salary could amount to as much as 14, 352.

Die Baxter railcar M.21 at St Valery Canal in 1955.

. . . Two goods wagons in a siding gave an air of activity, but closer inspection revealed that they were the home of the station master's rabbits and doves! . . . When I returned the next morning from Cayeux, the station master's young daughter boarded the railcar at St Valery, carrying one of the rabbits, very much alive, in her arms!

Notwithstanding this image of rural peace, Trevor Rowe conveys an overall impression of a busy railway, at least during the summer: 'At the height of the summer season [the diesel-hauled] train may be crammed full, and the conflicting interchange crowds surging in the joint booking hall [at Noyelles] are apt to get rather confused with each other'. At Le Crotoy he observed that 'The crowds [leaving the train] make their way off through the town to the beach, but one or two stop for a drink at the Café du Tortillard opposite the station', while 'Cayeux-Brighton is quite a busy seaside resort', and 'to judge by the talk in the [Cayeux-bound] railcar many of the passengers had come from Paris to spend their holidays there'.

In their final years of active service, culminating in 1957, the steam locomotives were largely confined to sugar beet trains. Thereafter only No. 3.532 was kept in reserve. The very last steam working was a Fédération des Amis des Chemins de Fer Secondaires (FACS) special on 5th April, 1959, behind SACM No. 3.532; the steam locomotives were scrapped in 1961 and 1962. Sadly, an attempt to save No. 3.532 was too late, although Corpet 0-6-0T *La Scarpe* (1087/1907) continued to work at the Sociéte F. Beghin sugar beet *raperie* at Lanchères until 1965. (This locomotive had been acquired from the Sucrerie d'Arras, Longueval, Somme, as recently as October 1951. The *raperie* closed after the 1965-66 season; the Orenstein & Koppel 0-6-0T and wagons were scrapped but the Corpet was saved, thanks to CFBS founding member C-E. Girode; it is now at the Tramway Touristique de l'Aisne in Belgium.)

Already in 1955 some of the metre gauge steam locomotives were in retirement at St Valery Canal.   *C.H.A. Townley*

Holiday-makers disembarking from a railcar at Cayeux. A picture postcard from the 1950s (?)
LUC/Collection R. Arzul

Blanc Misseron Tubize 2-6-0T No. 3.661 at St Valery Canal in 1955.
M. Rifault/Collection J-L Rochaix, reproduced with the permission of BVA

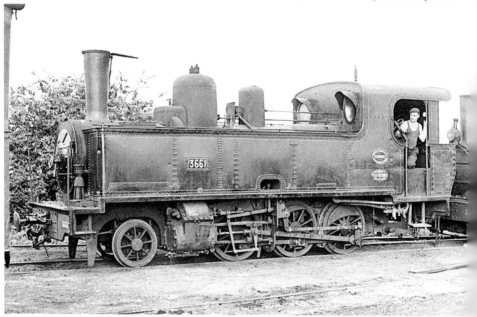

The situation in 1958

As elsewhere in the post-war years, railways in this area suffered from competition from the roads. By 1958 the former Réseau de la Somme - which at its height had comprised some 340 km of metre gauge line - had almost disappeared, with the exception of the three lines connecting with the main line at Noyelles, that is, the 'Réseau des Bains de Mer' (two lines) and the line to Forest l'Abbaye. Passenger services on the latter had ceased in 1951, but sugar beet continued to be carried until 1964. The track was lifted in 1967. The 'Réseau des Bains de Mer' was saved from early closure by its holiday-makers - the 'sea bathers' who gave it its name. An article published in the French journal *La Vie du Rail* in 1958 provides an assessment of the 'Réseau des Bains de Mer' at a pivotal moment in its history, a time when the line was so busy that observers could still be tempted to be confident about its future. Some 150,000 passengers used the 'Réseau des Bains de Mer' annually, of whom 90,000 travelled in the holiday season (15th June-15th September); the article conjures up a picture of between 1,200 and 1,500 people arriving by main line train at Noyelles at peak times, with quantities of luggage, and one of the accompanying photographs shows a crowd three to four deep waiting for metre gauge trains at Noyelles (one hopes that they were not all expecting to get into the single railcar which is visible in the background).

In addition, in 1958 some 50,000-55,000 tons of freight were still being carried per year, including some 35,000-40,000 tons of sugar beet (and pulp), and 10,000 tons of *galets*. The operational stock of motive power, according to *La Vie du Rail*, comprised three of the original De Dion railcars, the more recently acquired De Dion railcar M-41, one VFIL railcar, two trailing cars (used in the holiday period), and the two VFIL diesel locomotives. Passenger stock, other than the railcars and trailing cars, comprised 19 Manage bogie coaches with balconies (described by Bryan Morgan as having 'just enough floral decoration to remind you that the pleasure-beaches are near'), complemented by three *fourgons* (baggage vans). The stock of wagons totalled 310 items: 61 box wagons, 78 flat wagons, and 171 open wagons. Towards the end of the 1950s the body was removed from a coach (number unknown) and the chassis was used for transporting containers of powdered *galets* from the Sanson works, just beyond the station at Cayeux; at Noyelles the containers were transferred to SNCF wagons. (This chassis is now part of carriage No. 10507.)

La Vie du Rail describes the operations in 1958 as follows. On each line railcars provided two return trips out of season, three in the summer. For peak passenger traffic, carriages hauled by a diesel locomotive were utilised. One mixed train travelled daily between Noyelles, St Valery, and Cayeux. Every day one or two trains of standard gauge wagons were hauled by a metre gauge locomotive between Noyelles and St Valery Canal or port. In the sugar beet season, trains brought beet from the fields to the *raperie* at Lanchères.

La Vie du Rail concluded with cautious optimism. It noted that 'the operation of the entire system is carried out with strict economy, but not at the expense of efficient running', drawing attention to the fact that the St Valery-Cayeux line had been relaid a year or so previously and observing that each year the stations

A train load of sugar beet at Forest l'Abbaye, waiting to be brought to the *raperie* at Lanchères. One of the diesel locomotives can be glimpsed behind the wagons, November 1961.

Collection R. Arzul

Diesel locomotive No. 352 at Cayeux in September 1963.

M. Rifault/Collection J-L Rochaix, reproduced with the permission of BVA

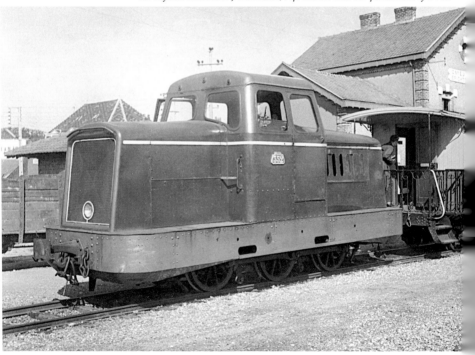

were freshened up with a coat of paint. It noted too the value of the 'Réseau des Bains de Mer' in enabling the many holiday-makers visiting the area to complete their journey by rail; local bus services could not be expected to cope with such numbers. Finally it offered the forecast that 'Dynamic management, modernisation, rationalisation and strict economy may well take it [the railway] to the end of its 99-year concession'. What it did not foresee, or chose to ignore, was the transport revolution which was about to happen - the growth of ownership of private cars - which was to all but finish off the 'Réseau des Bains de Mer'; to survive, it would have to re-invent itself as a 'tourist railway', a novelty for the enjoyment of visitors arriving by car.

One event which took place in 1958 almost seems to symbolise a will to keep the railway going against the odds. The fire which destroyed railcar M-21 at Cayeux also razed the locomotive shed. The latter, however, was quickly rebuilt.

The CFTA and the years before closure

In 1960 the SE merged with the Compagnie des Chemins de Fer Secondaires; the organisation which resulted from this merger was called the Compagnie Générale de Chemins de Fer et de Transports Automobiles (CFTA) and exists today as a subsidiary of the Vivendi group. The CFTA inherited responsibility for operating the 'Réseau des Bains de Mer', and this resulted in a change of livery from the SE's green to red and cream. It was in 1960 that W.J.K. Davies visited the line; his revised version of Trevor Rowe's article recorded that 'All services are now dieselised', and that four derelict locomotives, two 0-6-2Ts and two 2-6-0Ts, could be seen in the yard at St Valery Canal. In his book *French Minor Railways*, Davies wrote of how he arrived on the scene just after 'complete dieselization' had set in; four steam locomotives had gone, and four remained on the scraproad at St Valery Canal. (They were scrapped in 1962.) His initial disappointment, exacerbated by heavy rain, lifted when the weather cleared to reveal a railway which was 'still playing its part as a local communications system . . . so that the railcars, doing a brisk parcels traffic, and the mixed trains were accepted as part of the life of the countryside'. Moreover, the 'battered or newly overhauled railcars had a character of their own', while 'the station master at St Valery was justly proud of his very pleasant new station building, replacing one destroyed during the war'. On this last point Davies was mistaken; the elegant St Valery Ville station had been built in 1937; it was the depot at St Valery Canal which had been destroyed in 1944, by a fire probably started by an incendiary bomb. Work on replacing it began in 1945, but the larger building which is still in use (and which has been extended) was erected in 1947. (Plans survive in the Département archives at Amiens.)

Both goods and passenger traffic declined from the middle of the 1960s; the winter 1962-63 timetable (as published in the *Chaix Nord*) shows just two daily services on each line in each direction - a 6.12 from Cayeux and a 6.32 from Le Crotoy (both railcars), connecting at Noyelles for the Paris train (due in Paris at 10.22), a 15.30 locomotive-hauled train from Cayeux, and a 16.10 railcar from Le Crotoy, again connecting with a train due in Paris at 19.07; a railcar and a

English visitors. Diesel locomotive No. 352 departs from Noyelles with a *Railway Magazine*/Locomotive Club of Great Britain special, 15th May, 1966.   *Brian Stephenson*

After visiting Cayeux, the *Railway Magazine*/Locomotive Club of Great Britain special is seen approaching Noyelles, 15th May, 1966. The entire train is in the CFTA's red and cream livery.
                                                                                    Brian Stephenson

locomotive-hauled train at midday from Noyelles, meeting the 8.54 from Paris, and 17.04 and 17.05 railcars from Noyelles meeting the 14.24 from Paris. (Extra trains were scheduled for Mondays, Saturdays, Sundays and public holidays.)

As ever, simultaneous arrivals and departures from Noyelles, coinciding with arrivals and departures on the main line, remain a feature of the timetable. The sugar beet refinery at Lanchères closed in 1964. Until the very end the Madot restaurant at Le Crotoy used the railway to bring to its tables types of shellfish not available locally. A special vehicle, largely open but with an enclosed section, seemingly built on a flat wagon, was hauled by the railcars on the Le Crotoy line; special boxes, or *coffres*, containing shellfish were carried in the open section (*see page 162*). Closure of the Le Crotoy line was implemented, in spite of local opposition, with effect from 31st December, 1969. CFTA operations continued for three more years on the Cayeux line. *Galets* were carried on this line until the end of 1970. It finally closed on 31st December, 1972, the last train being railcar M-42 which returned to St Valery Canal empty but for the *Chef d'exploitation* and the *Chef de dépôt*.

During this critical period the 'Réseau des Bains de Mer' was visited by several English enthusiasts. Peter Lemmey visited the line with others on 29th September, 1968, during a tour organised by the Locomotive Club of Great Britain, just three months before the Le Crotoy branch was to close. He recalls getting off the steam-hauled main line train at Noyelles to find their 'special' waiting - M-42 railcar and a bogie coach, painted 'in the latest cherry red/beige livery'. Accompanied by the line's 'directeur' and daughter, they set out for St Valery, halting at St Valery Canal to inspect the three diesel locomotives inside the depot 'and the antique Verney railcar M-31 settling deeper into the long grass outside year by year'. At Cayeux 'railcar M-40 waited in its shed before working the service train which was to follow ours back to the junction'. On the return journey, they stopped to inspect 'the derelict locos near St Valery', even then 'rusty almost beyond identification' (Lemmey speculated that they might have come 'from the Aive-Rimeux-Beck line'). Back at Noyelles, the party were able to see 'the railcar arrivals from Le Crotoy and Cayeux flank our M-42 . . . while over the fence 'K' class Pacifics and 'R' class Mikados steamed past on the main line', before their train arrived from Abbeville.

In an evocative article published in 1970, Trevor Griffin also recalls arriving behind a steam locomotive at Noyelles where he was

. . . shepherded across the tracks to the station building. Here I asked for a return to Saint-Valery but was told that I could only have a single since this was a 'Chemin de Fer Economique'! . . . I was in fact given two tickets, an SNCF one for the section to Saint-Valery-Canal and a cruder CFTA one for the section thence to Saint-Valery-Ville.

Trevor promptly got onto the wrong one of two railcars, but was redirected by the driver who checked his ticket. The Le Crotoy railcar then left two minutes before the one for St Valery, which was:

. . . packed with locals and their paraphernalia. The excited chatter, together with a depths of Hell roar from the engine, made the experience unforgettable and one sensed that the passengers all knew one another, but they were not averse to strangers for I was

Simultaneous arrival at Noyelles. Railcars M-42 and M-43, the former being the 15.36 from Cayeux and the latter the 16.09 from Le Crotoy, approaching Noyelles for a 16.26 arrival on 15th May, 1966.   *Brian Stephenson*

M-42 and M-43 after arrival at Noyelles, 15th May, 1966.   *Brian Stephenson*

VFIL railcar M-43 at St Valery Ville, October 1969.
M. Rifault/Collection J-L Rochaix, reproduced with the permission of BVA

A diesel-hauled mixed train for Noyelles crossing the canal lock at St Valery, October 1969.
J-L Rochaix, reproduced with the permission of BVA

VFIL railcar M-42 on the level crossing shortly after leaving Le Crotoy on a misty day in October 1969.   *J-L Rochaix, reproduced with the permission of BVA*

VFIL railcar M-42 at Le Crotoy, October 1969.

J-L Rochaix, reproduced with the permission of BVA

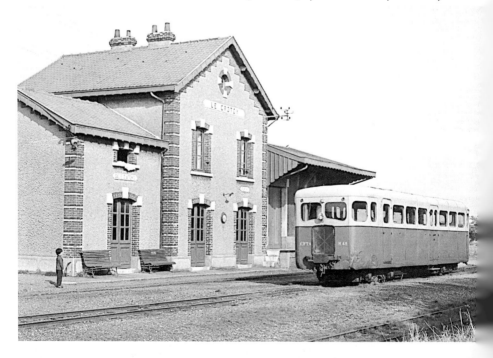

greeted with smiles as they made room for me. The interior livery of a sickly green was rather garish, with close packed yellow wooden seats, while a large yellow poster advertising a festival obscured one window of a partition which was, incidentally, oscillating independently of the car body.

Alighting at St Valery Ville, Trevor followed the mixed gauge tracks onto the quay, noting 'a platelayer's nightmare, a four-rail three-way stub point'. After settling into his hotel, he walked back to St Valery Canal where 'passengers are catered for by a simple shelter with a duplicated timetable sheet, and some semi-derelict buildings including an inexplicably enormous Gents'. The explanation, surely, is that he did not notice that the same building incorporates a *Dames* (today the only functioning toilet of the two, used more or less exclusively by male staff and volunteers) and other rooms. He did spot railcar M-31, evidently out of use, and 'hidden in the bushes a crane bearing the SE name in full on a cast plate'.

The next morning Trevor arrived at St Valery Ville 'to purchase the two tickets necessary for the trip to Noyelles . . .'

I noticed that two rather grubby vans, reminiscent of chicken coops on wheels, had appeared, mushroom-like, in the yard overnight. With the arrival of the railcar from Cayeux imminent, the Chef de Gare wound the handle which, by an arrangement of chains, should have operated the crossing barriers at the west of the station.

There was something wrong, however, for no sooner had he turned his head, than the barriers lifted about 30 degrees of their own accord. Muttering, he returned and wound again, but it was no use, and eventually he gave up.

After riding to Noyelles on a quieter railcar, Trevor changed onto the other railcar to Le Crotoy: 'The track reminded me of that on Drusilla's Tea Cottage railway near Eastbourne in that it was completely invisible beneath the grass. It was as if one were hurtling along an overgrown footpath, every bump in the trackwork making itself felt through the springless wooden seat'.

Returning to Noyelles, Trevor then caught the 11.03 mixed train to Cayeux, comprising diesel locomotive, 'some ancient carriages . . . and a string of goods wagons'. Following the arrival of a train on the main line, the carriages 'began to fill up'; *en route* to St Valery, the mixed train 'made a more leisurely progress than that of the bouncing railcars, and the guard hopped from balcony to balcony checking tickets, whilst children screamed excitedly, revelling in this new experience'.

After lunch at Cayeux, Trevor returned to the station to catch the 13.07 railcar.

Eventually I was allowed into the booking hall by a rather straight-faced *chef de gare* who also unlocked a grubby and rather spartan waiting room, whose walls were covered with peeling posters. A little later he opened the booking office, in order to sell me my tickets, and when at last the railcar drew in the doors to the station were unlocked. All this was very comical, since I was the only passenger!

On departure,

I watched the driver start up and get into top speed; then, to my horror, he left the controls, and calmly walked back to where I was sitting. Having accepted his kind

VFIL railcars M-43 and M-42 at Noyelles, October 1969.
J-L Rochaix, reproduced with the permission of BVA

The metre gauge terminus at Noyelles in October, 1969. Two VFIL railcars and a diesel-hauled
mixed train.   *J-L Rochaix, reproduced with the permission of BVA*

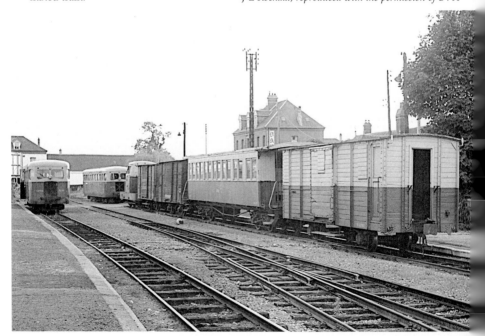

A metre gauge diesel locomotive hauling standard gauge stock on the embankment between St Valery and Noyelles in October 1969.   *J-L Rochaix, reproduced with the permission of BVA*

A diesel-hauled mixed train arriving at Noyelles in October 1969.
J-L Rochaix, reproduced with the permission of BVA

Diesel locomotive No. 301 approaching St Valery with a mixed train from Cayeux, April 1970.
J-L Rochaix, reproduced with the permission of BVA

Diesel locomotive No. 352 outside the depot at St Valery Canal, October 1969.
J-L Rochaix, reproduced with the permission of BVA

invitation to join him, we regained the cab, but the driverless railcar had meanwhile crossed about three minor roads on the level!

Some more passengers got on at St Valery, and 'the journey to Noyelles was completed in 37 minutes, compared with 50 for the mixed train . . .' Trevor concluded that

> . . . the friendliness of the driver was typical of many light railway traditions which the railway retains, and although it has no working steam locomotives, it has every other feature one would expect of a light railway, especially the way in which both staff and passengers take for granted the eccentricities that delight the enthusiast.

Such was the 'Réseau des Bains de Mer' during what so easily could have been its last years. Happily, even before the CFTA called a halt to operations between Noyelles and Cayeux, a preservation society had been founded and trains were running once more on the Le Crotoy line during the summer, and meanwhile the SNCF continued to use the section of mixed track - once again with standard gauge locomotives - between Noyelles and St Valery. An era had come to an end, but another was already beginning.

In the last full year of steam on the main line, a train hauled by a 2-8-2 stands on the northbound platform at Noyelles, alongside a metre-gauge railcar, July 1970. *Guy Pérève*

On the second day of its steam trials, Corpet-Louvet 0-4-0T No. 25 passes Morlay. Sunday 9th May, 1971.   *Maurice Testu*

A special train approaching Le Crotoy on 'Bastille Day', 14th July, 1971.
                                          Collection Maurice Testu

Chapter Eight

Preservation: A New Lease of Life for the 'Réseau des Bains de Mer'

The 'Réseau des Bains de Mer' - the 'sea bathers' railway' - always was a holiday-makers' railway, while also providing a service to local people and carrying local products. That is why these two lines, from Noyelles to Le Crotoy, and from Noyelles to Cayeux via St Valery, outlasted the rest of the metre gauge 'Réseau de la Somme', and it's why they were eminently suited to a new lease of life as a *chemin de fer touristique*. As previously mentioned, they were closed down on 31st December, 1969 and 31st December, 1972 respectively, although the SNCF continued to use the standard gauge rails on the mixed gauge section between Noyelles and St Valery for occasional freight. Happily, enthusiasts were on hand to keep these lines alive, and indeed were running trains between Noyelles and Le Crotoy even before the CFTA abandoned the Cayeux route. Their efforts were to be rewarded with success, although not without problems along the way.

Maurice Testu has paid tribute to a number of individuals who spoke against the apparently inevitable closure of the railway, among them Raoul Jacob, who wrote under the pseudonym 'L'Ami Rail' in the *Eclaireur du Vimeux*; M. Boucher, mayor of Lanchères; Max Lejeune, deputy mayor of Abbeville and president of the Conseil Générale de la Somme; Ernest Lecuyer, *conseiller général* of Nouvion; and M. Deray *conseiller général* of Rue. If the case for keeping the railway open was lost, yet their support surely helped to create a climate in which the railway could be preserved. On a more practical note, Max Lejeune was instrumental in persuading the CFTA not to send some of the Manage coaches to Corsica in 1973. Credit should also be given to M. Houard, *Chef de Dépôt*, who instead of surrendering to decline, in September 1970 arranged for railcar M-42 to be thoroughly overhauled in the depot, and who also ensured that diesel locomotive No. 352 and four coaches were given similar treatment.

C.E. Girode recalls a series of meetings which took place between 4th June and 16th September, 1969, involving himself, in several cases René Racine, other members of FACS, various local personages, and on two occasions M. Castelain, '*Chef d'Exploitation* of the Réseau de la Somme'. These meetings were instrumental in preparing the way for a preservation group to take over the Le Crotoy line. The decision to form a preservation group, initially called the 'Association Ferroviaire Picardie', was made on 13th November, 1969 and confirmed on 14th February, 1970; the Association officially came into being on 13th March under the new name 'Chemin de Fer de la Baie de Somme' - the word *touristique*, so frequently used in the titles adopted by French preserved railways, was deliberately omitted - and a first *Assemblée Générale* was fixed for 11th April. At that meeting the Treasurer, Hubert Hesse, drew attention to the need for money - at that moment only 112 francs 75 centimes was available. Subscriptions subsequently raised 6,570 francs. The initial aim was to preserve the Le Crotoy line on a non-commercial basis dependent on volunteers, with steam-hauled trains in the summer months. Local enthusiasts were joined by others from the Paris region (Geoffrey Nickson has noted that many of the preservationists at this early stage were people who

119

had known the railway as children - in some cases as a result of holidays in the area) and together they embarked on a period of intense activity.

The CFTA agreed to release its M-31 railcar to enable the Association to operate passenger services without delay (it was planned to commence on 'Bastille Day', 14th July). However, the Prefect declined to approve the commencement of passenger-carrying operations until further consideration could be given to the project, thus effectively postponing the re-opening of the Le Crotoy line until the following year. For the time being the M-31 stayed where it was; it was finally transferred on 8th July, 1971.

On 10th September (according to the Association's first newsletter; I have seen the 11th cited in a later source) a first batch of rolling stock released by the CFTA was moved from St Valery Canal to Le Crotoy. The train comprised coach No. 10502, *fourgon* No. 852, a box wagon, and a side wagon. These vehicles were pushed by diesel locomotive No. 351 so that the locomotive would not be trapped and prevented from returning if the train derailed between Noyelles and Le Crotoy! At each level crossing the train stopped and a M. Racine excavated the gap on the inside of the rail with a trowel. At Le Crotoy there was a minor accident: the door of the shed was not opened wide enough to admit the coach; the resulting collision was unfortunately featured in a story in the local press, in consequence of which both CFTA and CFBS personnel were reprimanded by the Préfecture for undertaking the day's manoeuvres without authorisation.

The CFBS was faced with two major tasks. The track needed and received immediate attention, although to begin with there were just two pickaxes, one shovel, one fork, and a wheelbarrow. Secondly, the Association needed to find a steam locomotive. It soon succeeded, thanks to the FACS. It was shortly after the events of 10th September that three CFBS members went to La Chapelle Saint Luc, near Troyes, to inspect an important collection of metre-gauge stock, including five locomotives, which the FACS had recently acquired from the contractor Paul Frot (subsequently Plisson). The asking price of 3,000 francs for each of three Corpet-Louvet 0-4-0Ts restricted the CFBS to one only, although with hindsight two would have been a sound investment. The 29th November was agreed as the delivery day. When the day came, CFBS personnel waited in vain until dusk; on the way home, driving through Abbeville, some of them caught a glimpse of the locomotive heading in the other direction. It was unloaded the next day, a happy event witnessed by television cameras. This locomotive's first steam trials on the line, following renovation, took place on 8th and 9th May, 1971, just over two weeks before the last regular appearance of steam on the SNCF main line at Noyelles on the 26th May. This was a historic occasion - the first time that the CFBS ran a locomotive under its own power. The locomotive was coupled up to newly repainted coach No. 10502, and the train set off for Morlay, where it was intended to call at the Café des Huttiers. Unfortunately the crew had forgotten to take on water, and it became necessary to stop and organise a chain of buckets (*à la* 'Titfield Thunderbolt') from a river! This event was reported by the weekly newspaper *La Baie de Somme* in its edition of 15th May, 1971: 'What a surprise! passing motorists are no longer accustomed to seeing such a locomotive crossing the road. But it has to be said that every precaution had been taken to prevent a collision . . .' [my translation]

Authorisation to operate passenger trains was finally confirmed by the Préfecture of the Somme for the 1971 summer season. Under the terms of the agreement, the Association was limited to trains comprising no more than two carriages and a van. Although the SNCF granted permission for the Association's trains to run into Noyelles, the local bus company persuaded the Association to agree not to collect or drop passengers at Noyelles, an agreement which remained in force until 1986, although exceptions could be made for organised groups. This agreement contributed to transforming the nature and orientation of the 'Réseau des Bains de Mer', confirming the drastically reduced significance of the interchange with the main line at Noyelles, and ensuring that most passenger journeys began and ended at Le Crotoy (and later, at St Valery or Cayeux). Only in recent years has Noyelles begun to reclaim a little of its old importance.

Services commenced on Sunday 4th July, 1971 with a 14.30 departure from Le Crotoy, and continued on Saturday, Sunday, and holiday afternoons through the summer. Some 2,700 passengers were carried in this first season, followed by 5,000 in the summer of 1972. The return journey from Le Crotoy was timed for 1½ hours, with 15 minutes at Noyelles and a stop at Morlay to allow passengers to visit the Café des Huttiers and children to enjoy a pony ride under the trees. Also during 1971, no less than six more steam locomotives arrived on the scene, in varying states of repair, as did a *fourgon* and a coach. Two more of the ex-Paul Frot Corpet-Louvet 0-4-0Ts had been acquired in 1971 and a second one, No. 25, had been put into service that same year. Alterations required by the two active Corpets included the raising of the buffers so that the locomotives could be coupled to the carriages. These two locomotives, known as *'les Teckels'* ('the dachshunds') are low in relation to the carriages, which is not only unsatisfactory from an aesthetic point of view but also increases the likelihood of smoke swirling around and into the carriages, especially when the engines are running cab first. But they served the needs of the moment, being in excellent condition, simple to operate and maintain, and easy-going on the track while holding it well.

Meanwhile the closure of the Cayeux line had been announced. The Association's proposals to extend its operations to embrace the Cayeux line were called into question by an insufficiency of funds, experience, and volunteers, but the growth in passenger numbers in 1972, and an increase in membership, confirmed the Association's viability. On 8th July, 1972 the Le Crotoy line was officially reopened at a ceremony at Le Crotoy station.

The CFTA ceased operating trains between Noyelles, St Valery, and Cayeux at the end of 1972. Now the CFBS was ready to step in, but it did so in the form of a newly created limited company, the 'Compagnie des Chemins de Fer Touristiques et Industriels de Picardie' (CFTIP), which officially came into being on 17th April, 1973. The CFTIP was set up alongside the 'Association de Chemin de Fer de la Baie de Somme', to present a more business-like image to the world and because the constitution of a limited company (a *Société anonyme à responsabilité limitée*) made it possible to raise badly-needed capital. The initial capital comprised 23,500 francs, the result of selling 47 shares for 500 francs each; there were 16 purchasers. Even before the official inauguration of the CFTIP, an application was submitted to the Département, on 10th January, asking for the CFTIP to be authorised to operate the 'Réseau des Bains de Mer'. With effect from 1973, until 1981, the CFTIP, rather than

Work in progress on the line near Le Crotoy, with railcar M-31, February 1972.

Collection Maurice Testu

A works train, including trailing car R6, near Morlay in 1976.

Guy Pérève

Corpet-Louvet 0-4-0T No. 21 at Le Crotoy, 25th September, 1972.   *Paul Lenne*

the CFBS, was to be responsible for running the railway. But a bid to take over the freight traffic operated by the SNCF between Noyelles and St Valery was unsuccessful.

In the first instance, three *gérants* (managers) were chosen; M. Salmon took overall charge, M. Guy Lenne became responsible for the St Valery-Cayeux line, and M. Girode was charged with responsibility for the line between Le Crotoy and Noyelles. Unhappily, the 1973 season was not a huge success. Some 5,400 passengers were carried, with trains running between Noyelles, Le Crotoy, and St Valery and a few trains being operated between St Valery and Cayeux, but the season showed a deficit of 8689.02 francs, and thereafter relations between the CFTIP and the CFBS were troubled. Guy Lenne resigned on 15th February, 1974; in the following month a M. Goujard appeared on the scene, announced his intention of investing 400,000 francs in the railway, and nominated himself to the post of *Directeur d'Exploitation*, supported by M. Salmon. Understandably, M. Girode took exception to this, and wrote a long letter to shareholders of the CFTIP outlining a plan for rescuing the railway, and criticising Salmon for his part in the upheavals and for founding another association, 'les Amis de la Vapeur', which was a distraction from the objectives of the CFBS. (Its principal concern was apparently with the preservation of small standard gauge industrial locomotives which would otherwise have been scrapped, including an 0-4-0T, *Union*, from the *sucrerie* at Rang du Fliers.) Salmon responded with a letter of his own, dealing with Girode's criticisms point by point, attacking Girode for taking on too much as both a *gérant* of the CFTIP and Président of the CFBS, criticising the decision to restore the 0-6-2T Buffaud which he said used too much coal (his own preference being the 2-6-0T Corpet of which he was at that time a co-owner), and also hinting at scandal - referring to unsuitable activities at the station at Le Crotoy, he deplored both the unauthorised presence of young ladies with no clothes on, and the unexpected appearance of a *draisine* (motor trolley) on the principal line 20 minutes before a train was due to arrive.

A *navette* (shuttle train) hauled by an unidentified Corpet-Louvet 0-4-0T at St Valery Canal, 4th August, 1974.   *P. Hutchinson*

A train hauled by an unidentified Corpet-Louvet 0-4-0T pulling out of Noyelles, August 1974.
Geoffrey Nickson

The immediate upshot of all this was the resignation of Messrs Girode and Salmon from 22nd March, questions from the Département, and an extraordinary annual meeting on 6th April which accepted the resignations of Messrs Lenne, Girode and Salmon and confirmed M. Goujard's appointment. The latter decision was, by and large, welcomed by the CFBS, and the 1974 season took on the appearance of the calm after the storm. In 1974 regular trains were run on the Cayeux line, and a total of 6,055 passengers was recorded. However, M.Goujard had taken on more than he could cope with and only lasted one season before succumbing to nervous depression. In April 1975 he resigned his post. At the general meeting of 21st April, M. Philippe Quiot became the new *gérant* of the CIFTP. However, it became apparent that M. Goujard's appointment had never been confirmed in law; it followed that Philippe Quiot's appointment as his successor was also, strictly speaking, illegal, and the three original *gérants* briefly found themselves reinstated by default. One meeting followed another, until at last on 22nd June an extraordinary general meeting re-appointed Philippe Quiot as *gérant*. But it was too late to rescue the 1975 season, and as a result only a handful of special trains ran during 1975 (a year which saw the arrival of an eighth steam locomotive, a Pinguely 0-6-0T).

As if the difficulties of the CFTIP were not trouble enough, at this crucial moment in its history the Association was riven by another disagreement. The impasse was resolved in January 1976 by a division of forces: the CFBS (and CFTIP) retained its interest in the Le Crotoy and St Valery lines, running trains past St Valery Ville station onto the quay at St Valery, whilst a splinter group took on the route between St Valery Ville and Cayeux under the name Chemin de Fer Touristique de la Côte d'Opale (CFTCO). The March 1976 *Continental Railway Journal* announced somewhat tentatively, under the heading 'Baie de Somme':

This year [the CFBS] hopes to operate between Le Crotoy and St Valéry via Noyelles. On Saturdays, Sundays, and holidays trains will leave each end of the line at 15.00, returning at 17.00, the journey each way taking about an hour. On Wednesdays there will be a working from Le Crotoy, depart 15.00, to Noyelles and back. 0-6-0T 101, ex-CF du Morbihan, is on loan from FACS.

There is no mention of Cayeux. This suggests, but does not make explicit, simultaneous departures from Noyelles at approximately 15.30 and 17.30, a still familiar pattern. The locomotive referred to is the aforementioned Pinguely which had arrived in the previous April.

In 1976 the CFBS carried 5,240 passengers; in the same year a second Pinguely 0-6-0T appeared, completing a fleet of steam locomotives which was not added to subsequently until December 1994. However, in 1990 this same Pinguely and another locomotive, an ex-SACM 2-6-0T, were removed by their owners to the Musée des Transports de la Vallée du Sausseron at Valmondois.

In 1977, 7,300 passengers were carried by the CFBS. The CFTCO operated diesel-hauled services during two seasons, borrowing locotractor 351 and autorail M-42 from the CFBS, before it ceased activity in December 1977, following the departure of a key individual to another railway, and responsibility for the Cayeux line reverted to the CFBS. Now, in spite of ups and downs, there would be no looking back. In 1978 a record 20,717 passengers

A scene in the depot in the early days of preservation. This was the first occasion on which the CFBS had lifted a carriage from its bogies. The volunteers are (*from the left*), J.P. Vlerick, from Belgium, Maurice Testu, at the time of writing the Vice-President of the CFBS, C.E. Girode, and Jean-Marc Page, the present-day President of the CFBS. April 1975.   Collection *Maurice Testu*

Inside the depot in 1980. The locomotives are Corpet-Louvet 0-4-0Ts Nos. 25 and 15, with the Buffaud & Robatel 0-6-2T just visible in the background. The railcar is De Dion Bouton X-157.
Geoffrey Nickson

Chef du depot Guylain Moreau working on Corpet-Louvet 2-6-0T *Aisne* in September 1991.
Roland Arzul

In this more recent view of the inside of the depot, the author (Philip Pacey) is seen removing rust from the chassis of a carriage. The Cail locomotive is behind me (*on the right*), and Corpet-Louvet No. 25 can be glimpsed beyond that. July 1997. *Ian Tate*

Two views of track relaying on the Le Crotoy line, winter 1992.   *Roland Arzul*

were carried, thanks in no small part to the dedication of just one member, a retired person who devoted considerable efforts to publicising the railway. The figure of 20,717 includes a substantial number of tickets sold by the SNCF to school-parties; the number of such ticket sales recorded by the CFBS was 13,682 (or 13,65l, the figure reported to the Assemblée Générale in January 1979).

With the growth of passenger numbers, more carriages were needed. Most of those inherited from the SE via the CFTA were in poor condition and not all could be brought back into use, so seven vehicles were obtained from Switzerland: two four-wheel vehicles, dating from 1911, were acquired from the Chemin de Fer Electriques Veveysans in 1978; three, dating from 1893, came from the Chemin de Fer Yverdon-Ste Croix in 1981; and two bogies coaches of 1929 were obtained from the same source in 1984. The body of a magnificent ex-SE bogie saloon of 1889 arrived in 1974 and, after being restored and fitted to another chassis, is used for special occasions. Nine ex-SE/CFTA bogie coaches of 1923 remain. The days of trains limited to two coaches have long since been left behind!

From 1973, CFBS volunteers undertook an ambitious but necessary programme of track renovation between Le Crotoy and Noyelles. The CFTA had allowed the line to deteriorate; writing in 1978 Geoffrey Nickson noted that some of the sleepers had been in place since the opening of the line in 1884! Derailments continued to be all too frequent until 1976. 20 kg/m rails were replaced with 30, and in places, 46 and 50 kg/m rails. The complete relaying of the Crotoy-Noyelles line was finally completed during the winter of 1992-93.

Corpet-Louvet 0-4-0T No. 15 at the head of a train near Morlay. The low height of these locomotives in relation to the carriages (in this case, from the Yverdon-Ste Croix railway in Switzerland) is apparent. *Maurice Testu*

The section of mixed gauge track between Noyelles and St Valery was and remains in a relatively good state, thanks to the SNCF, who relaid it with 45 kg rail during 1974-75 and who continued to use it for standard gauge freight until January 1989. After the CFTA ceased operations, the SNCF kept two Y-7400 locomotives at St Valery Canal, one to haul trains from Noyelles and the other to work trains in the other direction, since there was no facility at St Valery for a standard gauge locomotive to run around a train. Subsequently a run-round loop was laid, and thereafter a single SNCF locomotive, usually a Y-8000, was stationed at St Valery. SNCF freight trains operated three times a week, primarily carrying *galets* and scrap metal. Exceptionally a BB66000 locomotive appeared on the line at the head of a breakdown train in 1987 when the resident SNCF engine derailed on a point at St Valery Canal. The following year, on the occasion of the centenary of the metre gauge 'Réseau des Bains de Mer', SNCF overhead electric locomotive BB22396 *Baie de Somme* visited the line where it was manoeuvred by ex-SNCF Y-2107, given to the CFBS in the same year by the John Deere company. The last SNCF trip to St Valery, with locomotive Y-7511 in charge, took place on 6th February, 1989. But the SNCF did not finally relinquish its interest in the line until it sold the trackbed to the Département with effect from the 1st January, 1993. The mixed gauge track will of course be preserved; nowadays it comes into its own at the biennial festivals of steam organised by the CFBS and based at Noyelles, when visiting standard gauge locomotives may make their way to St Valery.

The last SNCF goods train to run between St Valery and Noyelles, hauled by locomotive Y-7511, on 6th February, 1989.   *Collection CFBS*

Meanwhile, the St Valery to Cayeux line, which in 1971 was in a better state than the Le Crotoy line, having been renewed in the mid-1950s, was maintained as well as circumstances permitted by replacing sleepers at intervals; in 1978 Geoffrey Nickson (then a new member of the CFBS and perhaps inclined to look on the bright side) reported that it was 'still in good condition', but Frank Wakelam, who visited the line several times in the 1980s and early 1990s, had a different story to tell. On Saturday 28th March, 1981 he was a passenger on a train whose locomotive derailed on the Cayeux line; the crew tried to jack it back on, but the passengers had to be taken to St Valery by bus. Frank's unpublished notes read: 'Track on Cayeux line is in sorry state with most sleepers rotten'. Travelling on the line on Saturday 12th July, 1986 he records 'Stop made to repair the track near Hurt'. Nothing daunted, he joined the 15.36 train from Cayeux on Sunday 12th July, 1992: 'Apart from the English and one or two families the passengers were suspected of being the young ladies of the very young crew. Slipped to a standstill at road D2, but after several attempts with soil placed upon the rails made enough speed to cross the adjacent busy and fast D940'.

Although this incident could not be blamed on the state of the track, Frank reflected that 'The contrast between the heavily loaded St Valery-Crotoy section with the Cayeux line is immense. In [the] U.K . . . a real effort would be made to get traffic on the Cayeux line, and [bring] its appalling track up to standard, or it would be taken up to recover re-usable material, if any!' To which one can only respond: bless our French colleagues for not closing down the Cayeux line

Derailment on the Cayeux line, 28th March, 1981. The back wheels of Pinguely 0-6-0T No. 101 have fallen between the rails.   *Frank Wakelam*

The special train assembled for testing APO's 'duo' bogies at Cayeux, June 1978. *Maurice Testu*

A Matisa *bourreuse-niveleuse* destined for Ethiopia undergoing trials near Morlay, November 1985.   *Collection CFBS*

and for preserving the 'Réseau des Bains de Mer' in its entirety! When I visited the line with my family in 1992, we walked from St Valery to Cayeux on a Sunday morning with the intention of catching the train back in the afternoon; coming upon the track just outside Cayeux, we too were astonished by its dreadful condition, with scarcely a solid sleeper to be seen and many in an advanced state of decay; imagine our alarm after we had joined the train at Cayeux and the driver accelerated to what seemed an excessive speed along the very same stretch of track which we had just inspected at close quarters! However, the Cayeux line has received attention from track gangs during recent winters; the last stretches to be relaid, including the section we were horrified by in 1992, were attended to early in 1999. Will this herald the return of regular steam services to Cayeux?

Since 1978 the railway has been used from time to time as a test site for new metre gauge railway equipment manufactured by French companies; ironically, it was the imperfections in the track as well as the gauge which caught the eye of M. Guillaumin, from Les Aciéries de Paris et d'Outreau (APO), when he recognised the potential of the line for testing 'duo' bogies for heavy duty metre gauge rolling stock for export to Africa. Indeed, the track was apparently not imperfect enough, since additional defects were deliberately contrived to put the test train through its paces. It included a long tanker wagon, full of water, and an SNCF flat wagon, both mounted on 'duo' bogies, with *fourgon* D-10801 adapted to serve as a travelling laboratory. (This *fourgon* has since been redeployed as the ticket office on the quay at St Valery.) The train was at times hauled by two diesel locomotives working at full power; tests took place during May and June 1978, and might have been repeated had not L'APO gone out of business. Unfortunately, one consequence of the collapse of L'APO was that a CFBS MMX bogie wagon, one of two which had been sent to Outreau for restoration, was scrapped; the other one was rescued in the nick of time. In 1984 a manufacturer of agricultural machinery tested a *remorque de draisine* destined for export on the railway between Lanchères and Noyelles. In this case the testing equipment comprised nothing more sophisticated than a human passenger reporting his sensations and observing the movement of some small pebbles!

More recently, sections of track have from time to time received the benefit of the temporary but active presence of brand new equipment being trialled or demonstrated. Late in 1985, Matisa France, in the course of exporting a *bourreuse-niveleuse* to Ethiopia via Dunkirk, stopped off *en route* to test it on the CFBS and to train an Ethiopian railway worker. Again, during June and July 1992 a *flambant neuf*, manufactured by Matisa for the national railway of Benin, was located on the CFBS so that personnel from Benin could be given training in its operation. Over six kilometres of the line between Noyelles and Le Crotoy it showed itself to be capable of ballasting 300-500 metres of track in an hour to a sufficiently high standard to allow trains to travel at 70-80 km/h. The CFBS nevertheless limits trains even on this stretch of track to no more than 30-40 km/h, for, as they say, visitors should be given their money's worth!

After the peak of 1978, passenger figures dropped to 11,124 in 1979, in which year M. Gentel succeeded Philippe Quiot as *gérant* of the CFTIP. A further reduction in passenger numbers took place in 1980, when the CFBS, like other

The arrival at Noyelles of a new *draisine*, built by SOCOFER, for testing on the CFBS prior to export to Ethiopia. 2nd July, 1999.   *Philip Pacey*

The SOCOFER *draisine* at Noyelles, 10th July, 1999.   *Philip Pacey*

tourist railways, felt the effects of the economic recession and of an indifferent summer, while visitors were deterred by reports of pollution in the Bay, due to untreated waste water from Amiens and Abbeville flowing into the Somme, and perhaps also to fertilisers being washed out of surrounding farmland; bathing in the Bay was banned for several years, until 1988 at Le Crotoy and 1993 at St Valery. During 1980 10,100 passengers were recorded. The ill omens of 1980 did not deter Claude Chabrol from coming to the railway to shoot a scene of his film *Le Cheval d'Orgueil*. In 1982 the troubled history of the CFTIP was finally laid to rest; at a general meeting on 30th January, it was agreed that the company should be wound up, and as from 27th April the CFBS was officially confirmed as its successor in a new agreement with the Département and the SNCF.

Since then passengers figures have multiplied. Some 25,500 passengers were carried in 1984, when in addition to its regular afternoon trains the CFBS promoted trains specifically for groups in the morning and early afternoons, and advertised excursions, by train and coach, involving, variously, an open-air barbecue, a visit to the Parc de Marquenterre (an ornithological centre), or a ride *en carriole* (in a horse and cart) through the salt marshes at Cayeux. In 1990 33,700 passengers were recorded, and 41,700 in 1991, followed by a further increase, thanks to an eye-catching publicity leaflet with colour photographs, and to a first 'steam festival', to 43,500 in 1992. Poor weather reduced the numbers to 40,768 in 1993. But 1994 saw an increase to 50,501.

In recent years, the Association has gone from strength to strength, thanks not least to generous grants, notably from the Conseil Général (of the Département of the Somme), the Conseil Régional (of Picardy), SMACOPI (Syndicat Mixte d'Aménagement de la Cote Picardie), and DRAC (Direction Regionale des Affaires Culturelles), in recognition of its contribution to attracting visitors and enhancing their enjoyment of the area. The day-to-day operation of the railway has been underpinned by the employment of a number of full-time and seasonal staff. Restoration activities have been furthered by co-operation with local companies and educational institutions, the latter including the Lycée Professionel d'Abbeville where students, supervised by staff, have taken on several projects including restoration of coach 10507. The state of the carriages, in particular, is far better than in 1983, when Frank Wakelam wrote in his notebook (Saturday 10th September), 'the rolling stock was not good, a window fell right out!' Photographs which have been on the wall of the mess room for as long as I have been visiting the railway indicate that some of the coaches have been used as a background for fashion photography! The depot at St Valery Canal has been restored and enlarged, and a carriage shed has been built nearby; accommodation for up to four volunteers has been built into the attic over the mess room in the former St Valery Canal station building (accommodation having previously been provided in the station building at Le Crotoy).

Further changes to the skyline at St Valery Canal took place at the end of summer 1998; on the edge of the railway's territory, the long-disused chicory factory was judged to be unsafe and was demolished, while close by the CFBS erected a large hangar covering three tracks, to provide covered storage space for material awaiting restoration. In 1995-96, the station area at Noyelles, immediately adjacent to the SNCF station, was upgraded and a disused building may at some future time be brought into use as a booking office and waiting room, thus restoring to Noyelles something of its former significance. The CFBS hopes to establish a museum in part of the SNCF station buildings at Noyelles. The engine shed at Le Crotoy was scheduled to be rebuilt (unchanged but for the addition of facilities for engine crews at the back) in 1999-2000. At the time of writing, there are plans to upgrade the station and the surrounding area at Cayeux, as at Noyelles in liaison with the local authority; this may include reconstruction of the 600 mm raised wagonway which in former days facilitated transfer of *galets* from 600 mm to metre gauge wagons, and some kind of display presenting information about the town's industrial history. Whatever its final form, this project is to be completed by April 2000.

The steam festival, involving steam-hauled standard gauge specials converging on Noyelles, along with appropriate activities on CFBS tracks and a model railway exhibition at St Valery, has become a regular event. Steam festivals were held in 1992, 1994, 1996, and 1998, and another one is scheduled for April 2000. Passenger figures have continued to increase despite the virtual cessation, in 1992, of SNCF's promotion of tickets for school parties visiting the area, involving interchange from SNCF trains at Noyelles to chartered trains on the CFBS. In 1996 the CFBS recorded over 60,000 passenger journeys; this figure was surpassed in 1997 when the year's total reached 66,219, in 1998 over 78,000 passenger journeys were recorded, and in 1999 the total exceeded 82,000.

On 27th April, 1996, at the steam festival at Noyelles, the CFBS signed a twinning agreement with the Kent & East Sussex Railway, the intention being to promote both railways and to be in a better position to seek European funding. The Kent & East Sussex Railway provided a strong presence, including standard gauge 'P' class steam locomotive 0-6-0T No. 1556. Two years later, on 25th April, 1998, also on the occasion of a steam festival) a new agreement was signed with the Département, effectively conceding the operation of the line to the CFBS for the next 10 years.

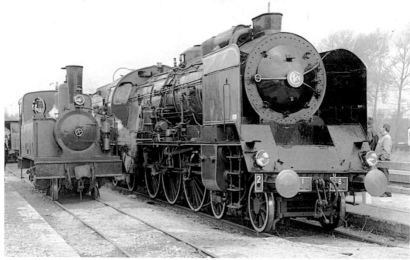

Metre gauge and standard gauge steam locomotives at the 1992 steam festival at Noyelles. Corpet-Louvet 0-6-2T No. 1 *Aisne* alongside a main line Pacific.   *Jean-Michel Arzul*

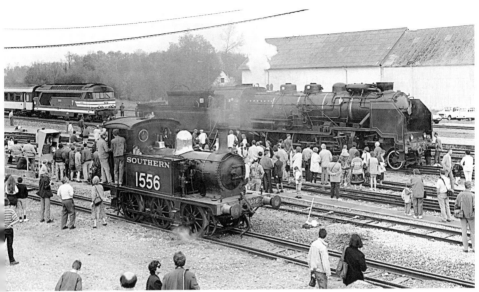

Standard gauge 'P'class 0-6-0T No. 1556 belonging to the Kent & East Sussex Railway in action at the 1996 steam festival at Noyelles. *Brian Stephenson*

Standard gauge 0-6-0T *Charwelton* from the Kent & East Sussex Railway at Noyelles on the occasion of the 1998 steam festival. *Brian Stephenson*

Above: Corpet-Louvet 2-6-0T *Aisne* running into Noyelles.   *Philip Pacey*

Right: Newly restored Haine St Pierre 2-6-0T No. 15 at Noyelles in 1998.   *Roland Arzul*

Below: Haine St Pierre 2-6-0T No. 15 at the head of a train between St Valery and Noyelles.
Christopher Nickson/Collection: CFBS

Chapter Nine

The CFBS Today

Motive Power and Rolling Stock

Steam locomotives in working order at the time of going to press comprised one of the three Corpet-Louvet 0-4-0Ts, No. 25; Corpet-Louvet 2-6-0T No. 1 *Aisne* of 1906; and Haine St Pierre 2-6-0T of 1920. The magnificent Buffaud & Robatel 0-6-2T *Beton-Bazoches* dating from 1909, which along with Corpet No. 1 had been the railway's principal workhorse for a good many years, was taken out of service at the end of September 1998 to be fitted with a new boiler which is now in place; it was also being given new tanks and a new cab, and will certainly be back in service for the start of the season, 2000. It was scheduled to be followed in the depot by Corpet No.1 which is also due for a major overhaul and a new boiler, while the Pinguely 0-6-0T is also out of action and awaiting a new boiler. After several years' restoration work, including a new boiler, the Haine St Pierre returned to service at the steam festival in April 1998. Corpet-Louvet 0-4-0T No. 15, out of action since 1988, was due to return to service in 1998 but was found to require a new boiler; it will have to wait indefinitely, since the larger locomotives now take priority. The third Corpet 0-4-0T, used for spares, can be found lurking in a dark corner of the depot at St Valery Canal.

An exciting project to bring a Pacific locomotive from Vietnam unfortunately came to a sad end late in 1994 when the locomotive in question was scrapped by mistake at Hanoi. However, money raised for that project was deployed instead to enable a most interesting locomotive to be brought back to France from the USA. This is a Cail 2-6-0T, built in 1889, one of six locomotives supplied by the Société Cail to work on De Lesseps' ill-fated Panama Canal project. This engine subsequently worked in Puerto Rico from 1891 to 1929; it was then chosen for preservation at the Henry Ford Museum at Dearborn before being withdrawn from the Museum's collections in 1977. Thereafter it was displayed outside a bank at Travers City, Michigan, from where it was brought to St Valery in December 1994. Although it is generally in reasonable condition, it has to be re-tubed before it can enter active service.

Two of the three diesel locomotives which came to the line in the 1950s are operational, as is a delightful little *draisine* or trolley dating from 1923. Of the surviving railcars, such a characteristic feature of this and other French minor railways from the 1930s through the 1950s, M-42 is being rebuilt off site, and Billard No.R-6, supplied in 1937 to the Tramways d'Ille et Villaine, but subsequently transferred to the Réseau Breton where it was reduced to an engine-less trailing car, is also undergoing long-term restoration, when time allows, at a local factory. A fourth diesel locomotive, BA12 from the Chemin de Fer du Blanc à Argent, built between 1942 and 1945, arrived in 1989, and a fifth, No. 824, built by Naval in Spain in 1966, was acquired by a member of the CFBS from the Ferrocarrils de la Generalitat de Catalune and arrived at St Valery in 1991. The CFBS also has at its disposal a standard gauge ex-SNCF diesel locomotive.

At Noyelles in July 1998, Buffaud & Robatel 0-6-2T *Beton-Bazoches* waits at the head of the train bound for Le Crotoy, while Corpet-Louvet 2-6-0T *Aisne* moves onto the St Valery train.
Philip Pacey

A Paris-bound passenger train on the main line is seen approaching Noyelles station from a metre gauge train hauled by Corpet-Louvet 2-6-0T *Aisne*.   *Philip Pacey*

A recent visitor to St Valery, and a notable attraction at the 1996 and 1998 steam festivals (though not itself steam powered), has been a Michelin rubber-tyred railcar, which formerly worked in Madagascar and is now owned by the Michelin company. This remarkable vehicle paid a first visit specifically for the 1996 steam festival; shortly after arrival but before the festival proper it was discovered that neither brakes nor clutch were working properly. Temporary repairs were made; following the festival, its departure was postponed so that more work could be carried out. In 1997 it returned to St Valery for a complete overhaul of all mechanical and electrical parts.

With the remarkable growth of passenger numbers in recent years, a lot of effort has had to be put into maintaining and restoring passenger coaches, and *fourgons* (to carry bicycles). The CFBS currently has some 18 passenger coaches at its disposal, including the splendid *Voiture Salon*, which has been classified as a *Monument Historique*. One of the nine Manage coaches inherited from the CFTA, No. 10507, the body of which was rebuilt at the Lycée Professionel d'Abbeville and by the Longhein company, also of Abbeville, has relatively recently returned to service; the Lycée is currently rebuilding the body of another of these coaches, No. 10302. The 'voiture de Verneuil' (ex-VFIL de l'Oise), actually owned by FACS, is also undergoing an almost total rebuild - only the chassis, and some seats and doors, will survive of the original. Two Decauville bogie carriages from Madagascar arrived on site in January 1998; they are in such poor condition that their restoration has had to be postponed. More recently two bodies of carriages of the former Buis des Baronnies-Orange line arrived at St Valery. After the closure of that line in the 1950s they were used as classrooms by a school for handicapped children at Orange; standing side by side on a low foundation and under a tiled roof, they suffered less than they might have done from the ravages of the elements. They resemble the Manage carriages, and it is hoped that they can be restored and put into service in the year 2000. Restoration of the ex-Seine-&-Marne *fourgon* was completed by volunteers in the CFBS workshop. In 1998 Guy Lenne completed the painstaking restoration of a *wagon à vigie* - a type of brake van on which the brakeman's seat is attached in an elevated position to the exterior of the body.

Operation and route

In recent years the CFBS has operated on Saturday, Sunday, and weekday afternoons (except Mondays) between July and early September, and on Sunday and holiday afternoons from mid-April and until late September, although trains between St Valery and Cayeux, which are diesel-hauled, run only at weekends and on holidays in the high season. Since 1994 additional operating days have been scheduled in April, May, June and September. 'Father Christmas' trains between Noyelles and St Valery ran for the first time in December 1996. The author is not sure whether to claim some credit for this! Earlier in the year, Guy Lenne, the editor of the Association's newsletter *Ch'tchot Train*, had asked the author to contribute a short article in French on the Kent & East Sussex Railway; it was written at St Valery, and Guy asked me for an explanation of 'Santa Specials'! He then added a footnote: 'Ces trains ont beaucoup de succès et sont

Track plan of Noyelles station, 1998

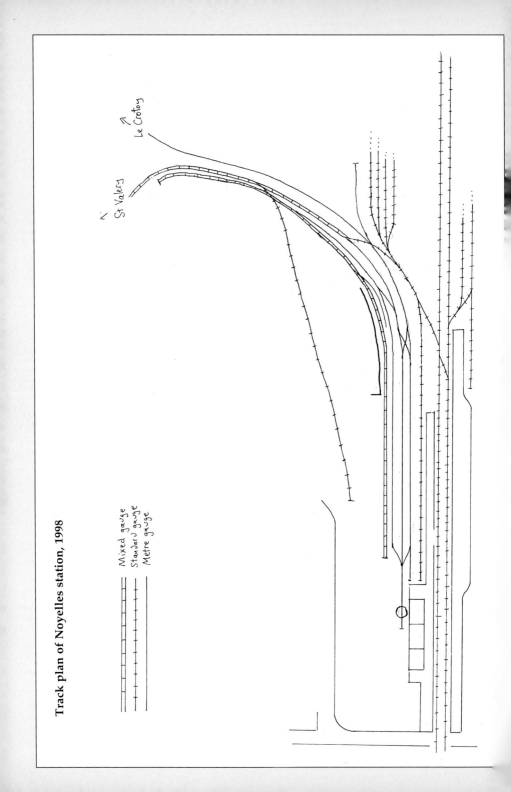

Mixed gauge

Standard gauge

Metre gauge

St Valery

Le Crotoy

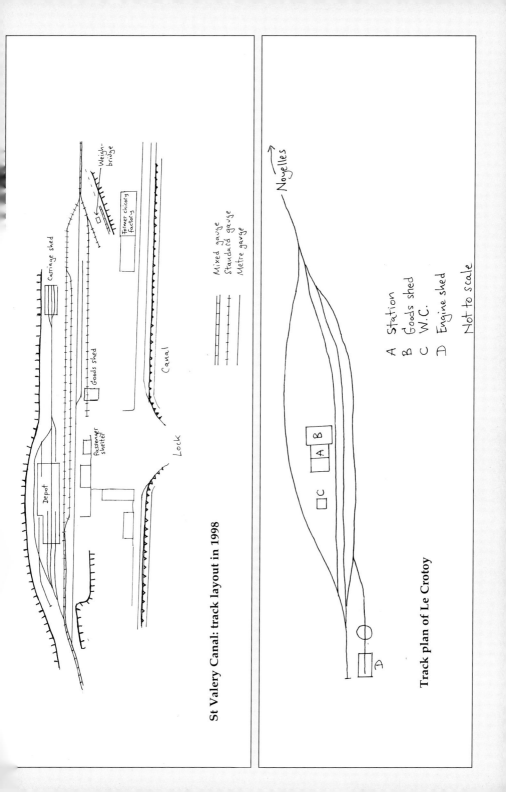

St Valery Canal: track layout in 1998

Carriage shed

Weigh-bridge

Former chicory factory

Goods shed

Depot

Passenger shelter

Canal

Lock

Mixed gauge
Standard gauge
Metre gauge

Track plan of Le Crotoy

Noyelles

A Station
B Goods shed
C W.C.
D Engine shed

Not to scale

A

B

C

A

Noyelles on Sunday 29th August, 1999. A diesel-hauled train of empty carriages has just arrived to collect passengers from the SNCF special train from St Quentin, Amiens and Abbeville, the diesel multiple unit seen on the left. At 10.00 am the sun is already hot; the SNCF train arrived first and the passengers are waiting in the shade outside the station. *Philip Pacey*

Departure from Noyelles: The Le Crotoy train on the left, hauled by Pinguely 0-6-0T No. 101, pulled out of the station first but the driver then waited for the St Valery train to catch up before opening the regulator, so that the two trains travel alongside each other for a few moments before the tracks diverge. The St Valery train is hauled by Buffaud & Robatel 0-6-2T *Beton-Bazoches*. *Philip Pacey*

aussi très lucratifs' ('These trains are very popular, and very profitable'!) (*Ch'tchot Train* No. 30 Octobre 1996) Unfortunately the experience of the CFBS so far has led to the conclusion that the operation of 'Le Train de Père Noel' 'est essentiellement médiatique' - that is, it is primarily of publicity value.

As noted above, trains can be chartered to run in the morning or the early afternoon. As at some other preserved railways in France, until very recently the regular service did not begin until mid-afternoon, in the expectation that intending passengers would wish to enjoy an ample and leisurely lunch! However, in 1997 a diesel-hauled 10.00 departure from St Valery was introduced on Saturdays, Sundays, and holidays in high season, as was a 14.15 diesel-hauled departure from St Valery to Cayeux; although 10.00 turned out to be a little early for travellers from St Valery, the return trip from Le Crotoy at 11.00 was popular. In 1998 this morning train was steam-hauled, leaving slightly later at 10.45. A significant feature of the morning train is that it makes it possible to travel the whole network in one day. A further development in 1999 was the introduction by the SNCF of a special train on summer Sundays (from 27th June to 29th August), departing from St Quentin at 08.08, calling at Ham, Amiens, and Abbeville, and arriving at Noyelles at 09.58 where it was met by an extra diesel-hauled train put on by the CFBS, scheduled to leave Noyelles at 10.00 for St Valery and Cayeux. The SNCF return train was scheduled to leave Noyelles at 17.40.

Trains depart simultaneously from the picturesque quay at St Valery, and from Le Crotoy, on opposite sides of the bay (which is not so wide as to rule out glimpses of puffs of smoke on the other side), at 15.30 and 17.30; arriving at Noyelles, passengers have the opportunity to change from one train to the other if they so wish before the two trains depart together, at 16.00 and 18.00. As we have noted, this simultaneous departure of two trains from Noyelles continues a tradition which dates from long before the preservation era, having its origins in the provision of connections with main line trains. It is, as other observers have commented, a narrow gauge spectacle without parallel, but photographers should be warned that in practice the Le Crotoy train sets off first, then slows down so that it can be caught by the St Valery train before the tracks diverge.

The line to Le Crotoy haunts the uncertain, shifting border between farmland and estuary; the train scuttles behind hedges and trundles over narrow dikes on minimal bridges before crossing a busy road - until recently with much whistling and gesturing on the part of the engine crew. Automatic lights and barriers were installed in the winter of 1997-98: crossing the road will never again be such fun. Within a few hundred yards, the train rolls gently into Le Crotoy station. At Le Crotoy the original two-storey building survives, combining the functions of station, goods shed, and station master's house; having functioned for some years as the CFBS headquarters, with accommodation for volunteers, the domestic quarters are presently rented. The original track layout is intact, and an engine shed, the home of one of the operational locomotives during the season, stands at the end of a single road.

From Noyelles to St Valery the railway runs for much of its length on the embankment, with meadows and pools inland and on the other side, the salt marshes of the bay, covered by grass and reeds and populated by sheep and occasional hunters who have dug themselves in by constructing *hutteau* - turf-covered hides - overlooking pools on which they float decoys. The embankment

Two views of Buffaud & Robatel 0-6-2T *Beton-Bazoches* at Le Crotoy, July 1997.   *(Both) Ian Tate*

Buffaud & Robatel 0-6-2T *Beton-Bazoches* at the head of a train which has just arrived at Le Crotoy, July 1997.   *Ian Tate*

Le Crotoy: the station building is on the left, the loco shed to the right of the track. The structure partially seen on the extreme right is a water tower serving the town. July 1997.   *Ian Tate*

Buffaud & Robatel 0-6-2T *Beton-Bazoches* crossing the embankment with a train for St Valery, July 1998.   *Philip Pacey*

The last departure of the day from St Valery crossing the embankment towards Noyelles, July, 1998.   *Philip Pacey*

At the approach to St Valery Canal (from the direction of Noyelles), standard gauge lines diverge to left and right while the metre gauge continues after a distinct lurch to the left.

Philip Pacey

Early morning at St Valery Canal: diesel locomotive BA-12 has hauled Corpet-Louvet 2-6-0T *Aisne* out of the depot. Here it will be prepared for the day's work.   *Philip Pacey*

Early morning at St Valery Canal: attending to Corpet-Louvet 2-6-0T *Aisne*.   *Philip Pacey*

Corpet-Louvet 2-6-0T *Aisne* makes its way through heaps of coal at St Valery Canal in April 1992.   *Roland Arzul*

After the day's work Corpet-Louvet 2-6-0T *Aisne* stands outside the depot at St Valery Canal. July 1997.   *Ian Tate*

Buffaud & Robatel 0-6-2T *Beton-Bazoches* crossing the bridges at St Valery with a train from Noyelles, May 1994.   *Brian Stephenson*

Pinguely 0-6-0T No. 101 crossing the swing bridges at St Valery on its way to Noyelles, May 1994.   *Brian Stephenson*

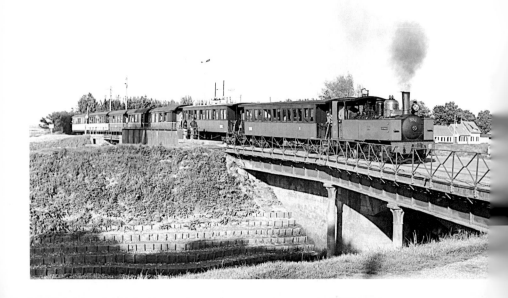

Two views of Corpet-Louvet 2-6-0T *Aisne* leaving the quay at St Valery with a train for Noyelles, September 1998.   *(Both) Ian Tate*

Corpet-Louvet 2-6-0T *Aisne* on the quay at St Valery, July 1997.   *Ian Tate*

Diesel locomotive No. 351 on the quay at St Valery, July 1992.   *Ben Pacey*

curves towards St Valery; the train whistles as it passes the depot at St Valery Canal, then whistles again as it takes a sharp bend before rattling across the road-rail swing bridge over the canal lock. The fireman jumps out to press a button beside the road which changes a set of traffic lights to red before the train crosses the road and swings right behind some houses, across another road, past St Valery Ville station (where it no longer stops), across the road again and onto the quay at St Valery. As at Le Crotoy, there is all the time in the world for the locomotive to take on water, and for the crew to enjoy ice-creams before running the engine around the train. What has life to offer more than this?

The line from St Valery to Cayeux is different altogether. St Valery stretches along the edge of a navigable channel, and up the side of a wooded hill; the railway, hidden in a long, tree-lined cutting where the branches meet overhead, bends and climbs around the back of this hill, passing under the only over-bridge on the whole network before emerging into open farmland. At this point, approaching the summit of the ascent, the train passes on the right the remains of the steam locomotives brought here by the Germans during the Occupation, and of a selection of rolling stock, grown over with trees and brambles. In the course of a long, gradual, perfectly straight descent, the line passes over several unprotected level crossings, some over busy roads and others over farm tracks; much use may be made of the horn as the diesel-hauled train and farmers on tractors approach the same point from different angles. Flattening out, the railway crosses another busy road and bends into the station of Lanchères-Pendé; there is now no sign of the former sugar-beet *raperie*, but a substantial agricultural depot dwarfs the characteristic station building. The latter is leased to a member of the CFBS.

Leaving Lanchères, the line turns towards the coast again, passing the halt, and a tiny roadside café, at Hurt; here an elderly crossing-keeper, who lives in the halt and performs this occasional duty voluntarily, holds up any road traffic with a red flag. Leaving trees and bushes behind in a final stretch across flat, open fields, the line turns into the outskirts of Cayeux and the trains comes to a stop at the station. Here again, the original two-storey station building survives, some of it is used by a local radio station. There has been talk of a long-term plan somehow to extend the line into the centre of Cayeux, close to the shingle beach, thus making it much more visible to holiday-makers, but whether anything will ever come of this remains to be seen. At the 1997 Assemblée Générale the suggestion was made that the line should be extended to Brighton (the Brighton between Cayeux and Le Hourdel, that is!). At the 1999 Assemblée Générale it became clear that an extension of the Cayeux line is likely to be envisaged within the context of the further development of the area south of the bay, led by the Syndicat Mixte pour l'Aménagement de la Côte Picarde; under the heading 'Projet d'Extension de la ligne de Cayeux' the minutes of the meeting record the unanimous approval of five motions committing the CFBS to support and co-operate with this project, which was reported to be 'en phase préparatoire'*.

---

* There has also been a suggestion for reviving use of a Decauville-type light rail system for transporting *galets* near Le Hourdel, in 'a version adapted to tourism' so that holiday-makers could also be given rides during the season. This idea has been put forward as an environmentally-friendly alternative to an average of 150 lorries per day, rising to 240 per day, on the 'route blanche' through the dunes. (See *Pour le Littoral Picard et la Baie de Somme Bulletin* No. 10 December 1996).

The station building at Lanchères. The building in the background is an agricultural depot.

Ian Tate

The station building at Lanchères, as seen from the road.   *Philip Pacey*

A diesel-hauled train in the open country near Cayeux, September 1998. *Ian Tate*

Diesel locomotive No. 3512 passing the halt at Hurt with a train for Cayeux. The crossing-keeper's house is on the right; the building on the left is a café. September 1998. *Ian Tate*

Of course, England is just the other side of the Channel, and just as St Valery is popular with the English yachting fraternity, so too it should be a mecca for English railway enthusiasts. An increase in English visitors was noted in 1997, no doubt as a direct result of the opening of the Channel Tunnel but perhaps also stimulated by the link with the Kent & East Sussex Railway and by publicity in the British railway press. For those with a car it is quick and easy to drive from the Channel ports and *Le Shuttle*. But for committed railway enthusiasts (the kind who choose to travel by train) there are two possibilities: ferry to Boulogne, where there is likely to be time to explore the old town on the hill before catching a train from Boulogne Ville; or *Eurostar* to Calais Fréthun, where in theory it is possible to change onto a train for Noyelles. In practice I have only found this to work on the homeward journey; inexplicably, some of the Calais-Boulogne-Paris stopping trains *don't* stop at Fréthun. If there isn't a connection to be had, then catch the bus from immediately outside Fréthun station to Calais Ville. In all cases, alight at Noyelles, wait for the train to leave, cross the tracks and make your way through the SNCF booking hall. If CFBS trains happen not to be waiting, well, you may find a café across the road (sadly it had been up for sale for more than a year at the time of going to press - there is a brasserie only just out of sight of the station beyond the main line level crossing), and buses for St Valery and Cayeux stop in the station yard. You are entering an enchanted country . . . a unique landscape complete with trains.

A very special occasion. The wedding of Roland Arzul and Emmanuelle Moy, 3rd July, 1999. The special train, hauled by Haine St Pierre 2-6-0T, has stopped on the embankment between St Valery and Noyelles so that the bride and groom can pose in front of the locomotive.   *Philip Pacey*

Appendix One

Stock of the Réseau de la Somme

Motive power throughout the SE's Somme network was provided almost exclusively by 0-6-2T locomotives until the 1920s, when they were joined by a number of 2-6-0T locomotives. Locomotives were stationed at depots at Abbeville, Amiens, St Roch, and St Valery, and on the distinct Albert network, at the principal depot at Albert and also at Acheux, Bussy, Doullens, Ercheu, Fricourt, Ham, Montdidier, Nesle, Péronne and Rosières. They were as follows:

SE No.	Name	Type	Works No.	Built	Notes
3.519	Athis or Abbeville?	0-6-2T		1886 or 87	a
3.520	St Valery	0-6-2T		1886 or 87	a
3.521	Offoy or Noyelles?	0-6-2T		1886 or 87	a
3.522	Cayeux	0-6-2T		1886 or 87	a
3.523	Le Crotoy	0-6-2T		1886 or 87	a
3.524	Beauval (originally Amiens)	0-6-2T		1889	a
3.525	Peronne	0-6-2T		1889	a
3.526	Montdidier	0-6-2T		1888	a
3.527		0-6-2T		1888	a
3.528		0-6-2T		1888	a
3.529		0-6-2T		1888	a
3.530		0-6-2T		1888	a
3.531		0-6-2T		1888	a
3.532		0-6-2T		1889	a
3.533		0-6-2T		1889	a
3.534	Crécy	0-6-2T	4.089	1889	b
3.535	Molliens-Vidame	0-6-2T	4.090	1889	b
3.536	Hornoy	0-6-2T	4.091	1889	b
3.537	Acheux	0-6-2T	4.092	1890	b
3.538	Bray	0-6-2T	4.093	1890	b
3.539	Ercheu	0-6-2T	4.094	1890	b
3.540	Dompierre	0-6-2T	4.095	1890	b
3.561	Amiens (originally Beauval)	0-6-2T	4.201	1889 or 91	b
3.562	Beauquesne	0-6-2T	4.202	1889 or 91	b
3.563	Fricourt	0-6-2T	4.203	1889 or 91	b
3.564	Forest L'Abbaye	0-6-2T	4.277	1891	b
3.565	Nouvion	0-6-2T	4.278	1891	b
3.566	La Picardie	0-6-2T		1892	c
3.567	Somme	0-6-2T		1892	c
3.568	La Manche	0-6-2T		1892	c
3.569	Montauban	0-6-2T	4.438	1893	d
3.570	Harbonn-leres	0-6-2T	4.439	1893	d
3.571	Bussy	0-6-2T		1897	e
3.572	Beaulieu	0-6-2T		1897	e
3.510	Montvicq	0-6-2T	3.954	1886	f
3.512	Ebreuil	0-6-2T	3.956	1886	f

Notes

a. Built by Ateliers Nord de La Chapelle.
b. Built by SACM (Belfort) type '66'. Similar to Nos. 3.519-3.533.
c. Built by SACM (Belfort)? acquired from the contractor who built the St Valery metre-gauge line?

d. Built by SACM. Type '71'.
e. Built by Ateliers Nord de La Chappelle. Originally numbered 3.601 and 3.602 and utilised on the Ercheu-Bussy line (l'Oise).
f. Built by SACM (Mulhouse). Brought from the SE's Réseau Allier/Cher.

The five locomotives which follow are not listed by Guy Pérève (see *Bibliography*):

SE No.	Type	Works No.	Built	Notes
3.623	0-6-2T			a
3.639	0-6-2T			a
3.651	2-6-0T	Blanc Misseron 345 / Tubize 1583	1910	b
3.652	2-6-0T	Blanc Misseron 346 / Tubize 1584	1910	b
3.661	2-6-0T	Blanc Misseron 371 / Tubize 1661	1910	c

Notes
a. Brought from another network (after 1923)?
b. Built by Blanc Misseron Tubize.
c. Built by Blanc Misseron Tubize. Brought from the SE's Réseau Nord (Groupe Nord), sometime after 1923.

Of the locomotives listed above, the following are known (from photographic evidence) to have worked on the 'Réseau des Bains de Mer': 3.521, 3.522, 3.523, 3.526, 3.532, 3.535, 3.537, 3.561, 3.615, 3.661. All are recorded by Guy Pérève as having been based at St Valery except Nos. 3.535 and 3.537. In addition, Nos. 3.519, 3.520, 3.528, 3.563, 3.565, 3.566, 3.567, 3.569, 3.571, 3.510 and 3.512 are also recorded by Guy Pérève as having been based for all or part of their time on the Somme network at St Valery.

Locomotives which regularly worked on the 'Réseau des Bains de Mer' were generally fitted with twin buffers as well as a centre buffer, to enable them to couple onto standard gauge rolling stock on the mixed gauge section between Noyelles and St Valery.

In the wake of World War I, during which the fleet of locomotives on the SE's Somme network was significantly reduced, four Baldwin 0-6-2T locomotives are said to have made a brief appearance, though not, to the best of my knowledge, on the 'Réseau des Bains de Mer'. Haine St Pierre in Belgium received an order for replacement locomotives after the war; these were delivered between May and December 1921:

SE No.	Type	Works No.	Built	Constructor
3.851	2-6-0T	1.304	1921	Haine St Pierre
3.852	2-6-0T	1.305	1921	Haine St Pierre
3.853	2-6-0T	1.306	1921	Haine St Pierre
3.854	2-6-0T	1.307	1921	Haine St Pierre
3.855	2-6-0T	1.308	1921	Haine St Pierre
3.856	2-6-0T	1.309	1921	Haine St Pierre
3.857	2-6-0T	1.310	1921	Haine St Pierre
3.858	2-6-0T	1.311	1921	Haine St Pierre
3.859	2-6-0T	1.312	1921	Haine St Pierre
3.860	2-6-0T	1.313	1921	Haine St Pierre
3.861	2-6-0T	1.314	1921	Haine St Pierre

Of these Nos. 3.851, 3.853, 3.855 and 3.856 are known from photographic evidence to have worked on the 'Reseau des Bains de Mer', although only 3.851 is recorded by Guy Pérève as having been based at St Valery.

Guy Pérève also lists the following as having arrived between the wars:

3.993	2-6-0T	One of 1.050-1.053	1905	Corpet Louvet.

but this cannot be correct. SE 3.993 was a 2-6-0T built by Decauville (3.993/1919); it operated on the Réseau Vaucluse. Corpet-Louvets Nos. 1.050-1.053 were built for the Réseau Seine Inférieure.

The four locomotives below arrived on the Somme network during the 1940s:

SE No.	Name	Type	Built	Comments
3.614	Le Pin	2-6-0T	1911	Buffaud & Robatel. Hired from the SE's Réseau Centre (Allier) in March 1942; subsequently purchased in 1945.
3.615	Molinet	2-6-0T	1912	Buffaud & Robatel. Hired from the SE's Réseau Centre (Allier) in March 1942; subsequently purchased in 1945.
3.510		0-6-2T	3.954	1886	SACM. SE Réseau Centre (Allier) until March 1943; after a brief spell on the Réseau Breton (where it may never have been used) was transferred to the SE Somme (Albert network) in November 1945; purchase finalised, July 1948.
3.512		0-6-2T	3.956	1886	SACM. SE Réseau Centre (Allier) until March 1943; after a brief spell on the Réseau Breton (where it may never have been used) was transferred to the SE Somme (Albert network) in November 1945; purchase finalised, July 1948.

Of these, 3.615 is known to have worked on the 'Réseau des Bains de Mer' and to have been based at St Valery.

Steam locomotives remained the only motive power through the 1920s, and their dominance was not seriously challenged for some years thereafter. However, in 1930 the SE introduced a number of petrol Campagne *draisines* for track maintenance work throughout its Somme network. Diesel railcars, in the form of two Renault type KAs, first appeared on the Somme network on the Albert-Montdidier line. Ten De Dion Bouton type NJ 4-wheel railcars were delivered in 1936 (De Dion Nos. 144-153, SE Nos. M-1 - M-10); they were followed by two more (De Dion Nos. 164-165, SE Nos. M-11 and M-12) in 1937. Of these, just three were located on the 'Réseau des Bains de Mer'. A De Dion railcar and a trailing car, which had been in service since 1935, were acquired from the Réseau de la Nièvre in 1939. This railcar remains something of a mystery; the trailing car was one of four De Dion type NO *remorques*, apparently all acquired for the Somme network from the same source (although documentary evidence for the purchase of the other three cannot presently be traced), Nos. R1 - R4. In March 1940 M-21, a De Dion Bouton type NR railcar with bogies, which was trialled from 1936 on the Réseau Breton, was brought to St Valery. It was subsequently destroyed by fire at Cayeux in 1958.

In 1940 the entire Somme network had at its disposal some 66 carriages, 16 *fourgons*, nearly 900 assorted wagons including 522 open wagons (2 axles), 126 vans, and 160 flat wagons (2 axles), and 3 break-down trains (wagon plus 4-ton crane) .

During the 25 years after World War II, several railcars and three diesel locomotives were acquired, in most cases from lines which were being closed:

• M-31 4-wheel railbus, constructed by VFIL at its workshops at Lumbres and acquired new by the SE in 1957.

• M-41 - M-43 bogie railcars, built by VFIL at its workshops at Lumbres in 1936. M-41 was transferred from the Flandres network; the other two came from the Persan-Beaumont-Hermes line. All three arrived in 1955.

• Two diesel locomotives (Nos. 351 and 352) built in the VFIL workshops at Lumbres for the Flandres network in 1951 arrived at St Valery in April, 1957. Rather than fitting these locomotives with twin buffers in addition to their centre buffer, a wagon fitted with twin and centre buffers and couplings was employed between the locomotive and standard gauge wagons.

• A third diesel locomotive, No. 301 (later 353) was acquired in August, 1960. It was built by VFIL at Lumbres for the Anvin-Calais line, and in 1956 had been sold to the Régie Départementales des Transports des Ardennes.

• In 1971, De Dion Bouton type OC1 bogie railcars Nos. X-157 and X-158, built in 1937 for the Côtes-du-Nord, were transferred from the Réseau Breton. X-158 was subsequently transferred by the CFTA to Corsica; however, custody of X-157 passed to the CFBS.

• R-6 *remorque* or trailing car (a Billard type A50D1 railcar *minus* its motor) from the Réseau Breton (this vehicle had previously worked on the Ille & Vilaine line); this arrived in 1971, at the same time as the OC1 railcars.

At some stage, whether before or after the war I have been unable to ascertain, a railbus trailing car (R5) was acquired, or, as I suspect, constructed on site, possibly utilising a flat wagon. It comprised a semi-open vehicle with a closed cabin at one end, and was used for carrying shellfish between Le Crotoy and Noyelles. Special *coffres* (boxes) of shellfish were stacked in the open section; other items could be carried in the enclosed section, protected alike from the elements and from the smell of shellfish.

Remorque (railcar trailing car) R5, adapted for carrying shellfish, photographed at Noyelles in 1955.   *M. Rifault, reproduced with the permission of BVA*

Stock of the CFBS

CFBS No. / Name	Constructor	Constructor's No. / Date	Date of arrival / departure	Origin/Notes
Steam locomotives				
0-4-0T 12 (Known as 'La Grise')	Corpet-Louvet	1589/1921	3.4.1971	Entreprise Paul Frot, La Chapelle-St Luc (near Troyes)
0-4-0T 15 (Known as 'La Marron')	Corpet-Louvet	1667/1925	29.11.1970	Entreprise Paul Frot
0-4-0T 25 (Known as 'La Verte')	Corpet-Louvet	1672/1927	6.3.1971	Entreprise Paul Frot
0-6-0T 17	Pinguely	39/1897	23.4.1976, removed 1990 to MTVS, Valmondois	CF de la Drôme
0-6-0T 101	Pinguely	165/1905	24.4.1975	One of four (Nos. 101-104) supplied to CF du Morbihan. Sold, along with No. 103, to the Forges de Gueugnon. On the closure of this industrial line, purchased by FACS and subsequently entrusted to the CFBS.
0-6-2T 3714 Beton-Bazoches	Buffaud-&- Robatel	1909	14.5.1971	A unique locomotive, ordered by the SE for its Réseau de Seine & Marne in response to a growth in traffic in 1908. Hauled sugar beet trains between Nangis and Jouy-le-Châtel until this line closed on 31st January, 1965. Purchased by a private individual on behalf of FACS, initially for a planned museum of minor railways at Verneuil. After this scheme was abandoned, purchased by an association intending to operate tourist trains on the CFD de la Lozère. Restored by the CFBS 1972-1981.
2-6-0T 1 Aisne	Corpet-Louvet	1097/1906	14.4.1971	Régie Département des Transports de l'Aisne. When this line was converted to standard gauge in 1961, bought by a private individual for the planned museum at Verneuil. Restored by the CFBS over a period of some five years, beginning some 10 years after its arrival; first steamed on the CFBS on 24th March, 1992.
2-6-0T 15 Noyon-Guiscard-Lassigny	Haine-St Pierre	1316/1920	30.7.1971	VFIL Oise (Noyon, then St-Just-Crévecoeur)
2-6-0T 3	SACM	7381/1924	4.1.1971; removed 1990 to MTVS, Valmondois	
2-6-0T ?	Cail	1889	12.1994	Panama Canal, then Puerto Rico, then Henry Ford Museum, and finally Travers City, Michigan
Diesel locomotives				
6w 301	VFIL Lumbres	1948	Inherited from CFTA	VFIL Pas-de-Calais, RDT Ardennes
6w 351	VFIL Lumbres	1951	Inherited from CFTA	VFIL Flandres
6w 352	VFIL Lumbres	1951	Inherited from CFTA	VFIL Flandres
? 14	CFD de Montmirail	1948	1979; departed 1990 to MTVS, Valmondois	Built on the chassis of Corpet-Louvet 0-6-0T No. 13 for the CF du Doibs; sold to Voies Ferrées du Dauphiné in 1954, then to Houillères de Bassin du Dauphiné à la Mure in 1964.

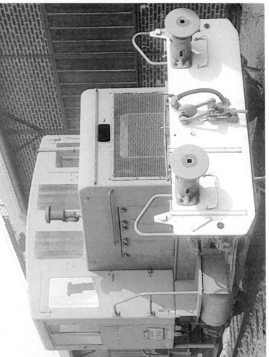

Left: Ex-FGC Naval diesel locomotive in the depot in August 1992.

Ben Pacey

Below: The only standard gauge locomotive belonging to the CFBS, ex-SNCF Y-2107, outside the depot at St Valery Canal in August 1999. Note the holes in the buffers, which are used by blue tits as nest boxes.

Philip Pacey

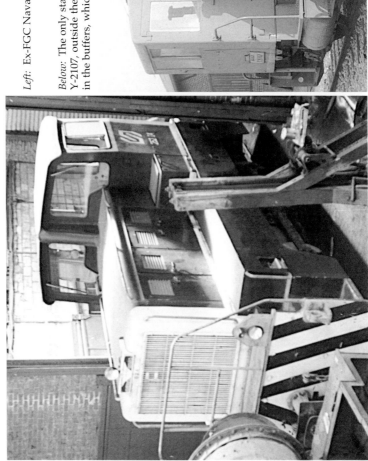

	Name	Constructor	Date	departure	Origin/Notes
6w	BA-12	Ateliers CFD de Neuillé-Pont-Pierre, (Indre-et-Loire)	1941-45	1989	Worked on CFD Indre-et-Loire from November 1945, then rented to Société Metallurgique de St Béron from November 1951. Sold to CF de Blanc à Argent, February 1952. Made redundant following cessation of goods traffic in 1987; acquired by CFBS, renovated and repainted.
6w	824	Sociedad Español de Construccion Naval [Spain]	1966	1991	Ferrocarrils de la Generalitat de Catalune. From 1966 and 1989 was used by the FGC for various industrial duties in and around the port of Barcelona. Made redundant following the arrival of more powerful Alsthom locomotives. Purchased by a CFBS member.
4w	Y-2107		?	1987	Ex-SNCF; given to the CFBS by the John Deere company of Fleury-les-Aubrais (Loiret)

Railcars, etc.

	CFBS No.	Constructor	Date built.	Date of arrival	Origin/Notes
Railcar, 2 axles	M-31	VFIL Lumbres	?	Inherited from CFTA	VFIL Flandres
Railcar, 2 bogies	M-41	VFIL Lumbres	1936	Inherited from CFTA	VFIL Pas-de-Calais, VFIL Flandres
Railcar, 2 bogies	M-42	VFIL Lumbres	1936	Inherited from CFTA	VFIL Pas-de-Calais, VFIL Oise (Persan-Ercuis)
Railcar, 2 bogies	M-43	VFIL Lumbres	1936	Inherited from CFTA	VFIL Pas-de-Calais, VFIL Oise (Persan-Ercuis)
Railcar, 2 bogies	X-157	De Dion Bouton	1937	Inherited from CFTA	CF Côtes-du-Nord (1939-56), Réseau Breton (1957-71)
Railcar trailer, 2 bogies	R6	Billard	1937	Inherited from CFTA	Tramways Ille-&-Vilaine (-1952), Réseau Breton (1952-1969?)
Draisine, 2 axles	-	Campagne	1930	Inherited from CFTA	

Carriages

Series 10500 (2nd and 3rd class), ordered in 1919

	CFBS No.	Constructor	Date built.	Date of arrival	Origin/Notes
Coach, 2 bogies	AB 10501	Manage	1921	Inherited from CFTA	SE Somme. Rebuilt 1995-96; in service. Varnished wood finish.
Coach, 2 bogies	AB 10502	Manage	1921	Inherited from CFTA	SE Somme.Restored 1992; in service. Green finish.
Coach, 2 bogies	AB 10504	Manage	1921	Inherited from CFTA	SE Somme. In service; formerly used as a trailer behind a railcar. Red and green finish.
Coach, 2 bogies	BC 10507	Manage	1921	Inherited from CFTA	SE Somme, then SE Valmondois-Marines. Body completely rebuilt at the Lycée Professionel d' Abbeville 1996-97; mounted on the chassis of a carriage (number unknown) the body of which was demolished at the end of the 1950s and the chassis used for transporting containers of powdered *galets*. There may or may not be some small parts of the original 10507 in the present-day carriage. In service. Varnished wood finish.
Coach, 2 bogies	BC 10508	Manage	1921	Inherited from CFTA	SE Somme. In service. Varnished wood finish.
Coach, 2 bogies	BC 10510	Manage	1921	Inherited from CFTA	SE Somme. In service. Green finish. Can be converted for use as a dining car.

Series 10300 (1st and 3rd class), ordered 1919

	CFBS No.	Constructor	Date built.	Date of arrival	Origin/Notes
Coach, 2 bogies	AC 10302	Manage	1921	Inherited from CFTA	SE Somme. Currently being rebuilt (work began winter 1997-98) with a largely new body
Coach, 2 bogies	AC 10303	Manage	1921	Inherited from CFTA	SE Somme. Not in service; dismantled March 1997. Privately owned.
Coach, 2 bogies	AC 10308	Manage	1921	Inherited from CFTA	SE Somme. Not in service and in poor condition.

	CFBS No.	Constructor	Date built.	Date of arrival	Origin/Notes
Saloon, 2 bogies	ABCDf 105	Desouches, David et Cie	1889	23.7.1974. Entered service on CFBS 30.4.1988.	SE Réseau du Centre: Allier-Cher This carriage was exhibited at the Exposition Universelle at Paris in 1889. The original chassis was scrapped sometime after 1953, but the body was saved and the carriage restored by the CFBS using the chassis of an ex-CFD Lozère vehicle.
Coach/*fourgon*, 2 bogies		De Dietrich	1894	Inherited from CFTA	Réseau Breton
Coach, 2 bogies	ABef4	Decauville		January 1998	Madagascar
Coach, 2 bogies		Decauville	1906	January 1998	Madagascar
Coach, 2 bogies	ABef4	Decauville	1906	1999	Buis les Baronnies-Orange; subsequently used as a classroom at a school at Orange. Bogies missing.
Coach, 2 bogies		Decauville		1999	Buis les Baronnies-Orange; subsequently used as a classroom at a school at Orange. Bogies missing.
Coach, 2 axles	BC 101	Blanc-Misseron	1894	6.4.1971	VFIL Réseau de l'Oise (St. Just-Crévecoeur). The 'voiture de Verneuil'; rebuilding completed in 1998.
Coach, 2 axles	BD 201	Schlieren	1911	2.1978	CF Electriques Veveysans (Blonay-Les Pléiades)
Coach, 2 axles	B 204	Schlieren	1911	2.1978	CF Electriques Veveysans (Blonay-Les Pléiades)
Coach, 2 axles	B 22	SIG Neuhausen	1893	5.6.1981	CF Yverdon-Ste.Croix
Coach, 2 axles	BF 26	SIG Neuhausen	1893	5.6.1981	CF Yverdon-Ste.Croix
Coach, 2 axles	BF 27	SIG Neuhausen	1893	5.6.1981	CF Yverdon-Ste.Croix
Coach, 2 axles	B 31	SIG Neuhausen	1929	29.6.1984	CF Yverdon-Ste.Croix
Coach, 2 axles	B 32	SIG Neuhausen	1929	29.6.1984	CF Yverdon-Ste.Croix

Baggage vans (*Fourgons*)

	CFBS No.	Constructor	Date built.	Date of arrival	Origin/Notes
Post van, 2 bogies	D 803	Blanc-Misseron	?	?1993 (reported as being 'en cours de rapatriement' in the 2nd [1993] edition of the guidebook to the CFBS)	CF Yverdon-Ste.Croix
Baggage van, 2 axles	D 10801	?	?	26.3.1971	SE Réseau de Seine-&-Marne
Baggage van, 2 axles		?		?1957	SE Allier, SE Somme; restored and adapted as a 'laboratory wagon' in 1978 by les Aciéries de Paris et d'Outreau (APO) for use on trains testing 'duo' bogies; in recent years has been used as a ticket office on the quay at St Valery.
Baggage van, 2 axles	D?	?	?	Inherited from CFTA. Sold to MTVS but repurchased in 1995.	SE Somme
Baggage van, 2 axles	K 11008	?	?	Inherited from CFTA.	SE Somme
Baggage van, 2 axles	K 11013	?	?	Inherited from CFTA.	SE Somme
Baggage van, 2 axles	K 12005	?	?	Inherited from CFTA.	SE Somme

	CFBS No.	Constructor	Date built.	Date of arrival	Origin/Notes
Vans					
2 axles	K 502	?		1979	Réseau Breton
2 axles	K ?	?		1979	Réseau Breton
2 axles	K 434	?		1979	Réseau Breton
2 axles	Kf 1590	?		1979	Réseau Breton
2 axles	K 603	Schlieren	1903	2.1978	CF Electrique de Gruyère, CF Blonay-Chamby
2 axles	K 1210	?		Inherited from CFTA	SE Somme
2 axles	K 1211	?		Inherited from CFTA	SE Somme
2 axles	K 1247	?		Inherited from CFTA	SE Somme
2 axles	K 1254	?		Inherited from CFTA	SE Somme
2 axles	K 1276	?		Inherited from CFTA	SE Somme
Brake vans					
2 axles	K?	?	?	1979	Réseau Breton
2 axles	K 2203	?	?	Inherited from CFTA	SE Somme
2 axles	K 2206	?	?	Inherited from CFTA	SE Somme
2 axles	K 2224	?	?	Inherited from CFTA	SE Somme
2 axles	K 2225	?	?	Inherited from CFTA	SE Somme
Flat wagons					
2 bogies	MMX3	? (German)	?	Inherited from CFTA	RDT Ardennes
Flat wagon built on coach chassis		Manage	1923	Inherited from CFTA: subsequently used as chassis for coach BC10507?	SE Somme
Flat wagons					
2 axles	M 302	SIG Neuhausen	1893	11.10.1976	CF Yverdon-Ste.Croix
2 axles	M 305	Pétolat	1905	11.10.1976	CF Yverdon-Ste.Croix
2 axles	M 309	SIG Neuhausen/ CF Yverdon-Ste.Croix	1893	11.10.1976	CF Yverdon-Ste.Croix
2 axles	M 310	SIG Neuhausen/ CF Yverdon-Ste.Croix	1893	11.10.1976	CF Yverdon-Ste.Croix
2 axles	?	Magnard	?	3.4.1971	Entreprise Paul Frot
2 axles	T 9209	?	1911	Inherited from CFTA	SE Somme
2 axles	T 9220	?	?	Inherited from CFTA	SE Somme

Open wagons (*tombereaux*)

	CFBS No.	Constructor	Date built.	Date of arrival	Origin/Notes
2 axles	L 205	Pétolat	1905	5.6.1981	CF Yverdon-Ste.Croix
2 axles	L 209	? (Italian)	?	2.1978	Ferrovia Appennino Centrale, CF Yverdon-Ste.Croix
2 axles	L 210	? (Italian)	?	5.6.1981	Ferrovia Appennino Centrale, CF Yverdon-Ste.Croix
2 axles	L 211	? (Italian)	?	5.6.1981	Ferrovia Appennino Centrale, CF Yverdon-Ste.Croix
2 axles	U 3305	?	?	Inherited from CFTA	SE Somme
2 axles	U 12087	?	?	Inherited from CFTA	SE Somme
2axles	U 13021	?	?	Inherited from CFTA	SE Somme
2 axles	U 13056	?	?	Inherited from CFTA	SE Somme
2 axles	U 14008	?	?	Inherited from CFTA	SE Somme
2 axles	U 14053	?	?	Inherited from CFTA	SE Somme

Skip wagons

		Constructor	Date built.	Date of arrival	Origin/Notes
2 axles		?	?	3.4.1971	Entreprise Paul Frot
2 axles		?	?	3.4.1971	Entreprise Paul Frot

Hopper wagons

		Constructor	Date built.	Date of arrival	Origin/Notes
		?	?	1992	Purchased from La Mine Orne railway
		?	?	1992	Purchased from La Mine Orne railway

Hopper wagon, standard gauge

		Constructor	Date built.	Date of arrival	Origin/Notes
		?	?	1997?	Purchased from SNCF

Cranes

	CFBS No.	Constructor	Date built.	Date of arrival	Origin/Notes
	G 9009	?	?	Inherited from CFTA	SE Somme
		Baume-&-Marpent	?	Inherited from CFTA	SE Somme

Appendix Three

Chu Tchot Train
by Gaston Bon

This poem is written in the Picard dialect; the English version which follows has been made from a translation into standard French by Guy Lenne. The poem is said to tell a true story; although an exact date cannot be confirmed, it seems that this event took place in the first half of the 1950s.

I

E' j'va vous n'in canter eune belle,
E'd quoi s'étotcher in riant,
Pareut que ch'train Tcheya-Noyelles
L'a foutu l'camp.
Un tchot nasu qui l'est richelle,
A yu l'ida tout in s'muchant;
Ed' patritcher chés manivelles
N'y a pû d'efant!
Mé v' la ti poé qu'chu train,
Y s'met tout d'un coup à démarrer,
In pétant comme un vieux boédet
Qui n'avanch'poé sans déblinder.
Chu nasu in'foat ni eune, ni dà,
Y sauve in bo a ch'tra caillas,
Et pis y met ses gambes à sin co,
Au grand galot.
Tandis ch'temps lo, ch'train y l'o d's ailes
S'invo o loue in s'déhotchant,
Sans meûme siffler à ches barrières
Qu'ch' est imprudent.

II

A l'pire ch'est pour no chef ed gare,
E qu'sin métier ch't'eune vraie passion,
Dire equ' jamoue ech'train y démarre
Sans s'permission.
Tout l'long de l'avoie al'v'là qui trache,
Après s'machine pis sin wagon,
I n'peuvent mi rester in plache comme un couillon!
In arrivant au 'Mont Rôti', no cacheu y l'éteut réduit,
On s'aveut poue qu'ch'est tuant d'porsuivre in sifflant
Quoère heura qui s'à poue inchpa, das chès orties
Das ch'bo cota, pour marthyr, on l'éreu trouva
Long ed'tchu fossa.
Tandis ch'temps là ch'train y l'a belle
S'invo o laué in s'déhotchant,
Sans meûme siffler à ches barrières
Qu'ch'est imprudent.

III

In imploya qui n'est paue bête,
O n'in voué quouère ed'temps en temps,
Y dit j'vo rejoindre peut-être à un tornant.
Vite y monte sus s'bicyclette,
Y passe à Hurt tout pédalant,
A Lanchères ch'est eune arbalette
Qui vo d'l'avant.
Juste à hautar ed Routhiauville,
Y l'appercheu ech'tchot train qui file,
Vin diu à l'côte ed d'Saint-Valry,
Sûr qui s'in vô y être ébarli,
Mais ech'tchot train s'arrête,
In r'martchant qui l'est porsuit par un'agent
Es su pama comme ti, tchot tiu,
Ej'n'in peut pû!
Amarre mé bié at 'bicyclette,
Ej m'invo et'suivre in ertchulant,
Coomo j'iro peut-être plus vite,
Qu'in m'in allant.
Troies jours après Tchéya in fête,
A vu r'passer echt' émigrant,
Que joie pinsez eune si boenne bête,
Equ'min tauere sans.

English version:

I

I'm going to tell you a good story
which will make you choke with laughter:
it seems that the train from Cayeux to Noyelles
set off by itself!
A naughty, crafty boy, hiding in the cab,
had the idea to meddle with the controls:
children aren't what they used to be!
And then, lo and behold! if the locomotive didn't start moving,
farting like an old donkey
which can't make a movement without passing a motion.
The boy neither stopped it nor helped it go faster
but jumped down onto the ballast
and took to his heels,
running away as fast as he could.
Meanwhile the locomotive went on its way
waddling along,
not even whistling at the level crossings
which isn't wise.

II

For our station-master, whose work is his passion,
it was the worst thing that could have happened.
Trains were not allowed to leave
without his permission.
Off he went, running down the track
after the locomotive and wagon.
He simply couldn't stand still
like an idiot.

Arriving at Mont-Rôti
he was in a dreadful state -
you can't imagine how it nearly killed him
chasing after the run-away, blowing his whistle;
it was lucky that he didn't come to grief in the nettles
along the way, where, poor martyr, he would have been found
sprawled in a ditch.
Meanwhile the train, forgetting its manners,
waddled on and on
not even whistling at the level crossings
which isn't wise.

III

Another railwayman - no fool
(such employees can still be found)
said to himself 'Maybe I can catch up with the train
when it slows down on a bend'.
Quickly he jumped on his bike,
passed through Hurt pedalling hard;
at Lanchères he accelerated like an arrow
shot from a cross bow.
At the top of the slope at Routhiauville
he saw the train rolling -
Ye Gods! - down the other side towards St Valery.
After it he went
but the locomotive, seeing the railwayman coming after it,
stopped by itself:
        'I'm as worn out as you are
        and now I'm not afraid any more
        Tie me to your bicycle
        and I'll follow you home.
        That way I'll go more quickly'.
Three days later Cayeux rejoiced,
celebrating the return of the prodigal.
What joy! Just think: such a good-natured creature -
how would they have managed without it!

Sources

The Archives Départementales of the Conseil Général de la Somme, at Amiens, include a lot of material relating to the 'Réseau des Bains de Mer', material which reminds us of the Département's role and close involvement with the railway. Much of the material comprises correspondence with and, in many cases, requests to, the Préfet, and is often accompanied by written information or advice sought by him from the SE and the Département's specialist staff, and his replies ; the majority of it is concerned with the construction and maintenance of the line and its buildings, rather than with day-to-day operations. Of particular interest are proposals from local industrialists to lay railway lines (usually of Decauville track) to link their sites to the railway. Some relevant material is contained in dossiers covering roads and canals, as well as railways, serving the various communities - Le Crotoy, St Valery, Noyelles, Cayeux, etc.

The archives of the Compagnie des Chemins de Fer du Nord, and also the archives of the CGEA (Compagnie générale d'Entreprises automobiles), incorporating the Compagnie Française de Transport Automobile (CFTA) which absorbed the Société générale des chemins de fer Economiques (SE), can be found at the Centre des Archives du Monde du Travail at Roubaix. An inexpensive (40 francs at the time of writing) inventory of those of the archives of the CF du Nord which are coded at 48AQ has been published:

Gille, Bertrand (et al). *Répertoire numérique des archives de la Compagnie du Chemin de fer du Nord (48AQ)*. Paris: Directions des archives de France, 1961,

But of course this can be consulted at Roubaix, as can an inventory of much more CF du Nord material coded at 202AQ. The CGEA archives are coded at 1996207, within which the CFTA/SE archives comprise Nos. 0365-0765. A great deal of other material on railway and industrial history can be found in this very welcoming archive, housed in a wonderfully converted former mill adjacent to the terminus of the Lille-Roubaix tramway.

The Air Photo Library at the University of Keele in England holds some five million photographs shot from Allied reconaissance aircraft during World War II. They include many photographs of the Baie de Somme region, some of which have provided invaluable information for this book. The photographs are organised chronologically by the date of each sortie; indexes permit the retrieval of photographs by area (defined by longitude and latitude). Researchers are advised to write in the first instance.

Bibliography

A select bibliography of French and English publications concerning the railways of the Baie de Somme is followed by lists of sources of information relevant to specific chapters.

French publications

Banaudo, José. *Trains oubliés 4: les Réseaux de l'Etat, du Nord et le Syndicat des Ceintures*. Breil-sur-Roya: Les Editions du Cabrie, 1983.
Le Chemin de fer de la Baie de Somme, [by] Maurice Testu, Jean-Michel Candillon, [and] Patrice Candillon. Breil-sur-Roya: Les Editions du Cabri, 1988; revised edition, 1993. 32pp. An attractive illustrated handbook for visitors to the CFBS.
Ch'tchot Train [previously titled *CFBS Bulletin*], passim. The excellent newsletter of the CFBS. Under Guy Lenne's editorship, this has increasingly published material of historical interest. The first of an irregular series of articles on the 'Histoire du CFBS', by Maurice Testu, appeared in No. 21, March 1994.
Dahlström, Marc. *La France à voie étroite*. Autoédition, 1989. Includes photographs of the 'Réseau des Bains de Mer' in the 1950s and 1960s.
Deleu, Willy. 'Le Sifflet du CFBS: au-dessus du pays de Somme'. *La Vie du Rail* No. 1357 10 Septembre 1972 pp.40-43.
Domengie, Henri and José Banaudo. *Les petit trains de jadis: Nord de la France*. Breil-sur-Roya: Les Editions du Cabri, 1995. 251pp. A magnificent volume, gathering historical information including photographs. The Somme region is covered on pp. 69-87.
'Le groupe des 'Bains de Mer' du réseau de la Somme'. *La Vie du Rail* No. 663 1958 pp. 16-21.
Neumann, Noël. 'En Baie de Somme, un chemin de fer touristique plate-forme d'essais pour nouveau matériel ferroviaire'. *La Vie de Rail* 23 Juillet, 1978 pp.4-7. An account of the beginnings of use of the CFBS for testing modern equipment.
Nickson, Geoffrey. 'Baie de Somme, an 10'. *Voie Etroite* No. 68 1982 (No. 1) pp. 3-13
Saint-Valery d'Hier: vie quotidienne à Saint-Valery-sur-Somme de 1866 à 1940. Abbeville: F. Paillart, 1985. Also similar volumes devoted to Le Crotoy and Cayeux.
Testu, Maurice, 'L'Histoire du Chemin de Fer de la Baie de Somme'. *Chemins de Fer Régionaux & Urbains* No. 273, 3/1999 pp. 4-26.
Villers, Claude and Patrick Delance. *La France à toute vapeur*. Editions du Chêne, 1999 pp. 50-59. Noteworthy for the magnificent photographs by Patrick Delance.
Voie Etroite, passim. Almost every issue of this splendid journal includes a report from the CFBS.

English publications

Allen, Peter and P.B.Whitehouse. *Narrow Gauge Railways of Europe*. London: Ian Allan, 1959. Although the Baie de Somme does not feature prominently in this book, it is - literally - its point of departure: see the Author's Preface.
Barnabe, Giles. 'Along French byways: useful items of light railway equipment'. *Continental Modeller* October 1993 pp. 386-387. Includes descriptions, photographs and drawings of vans and wagons preserved on the CFBS.
Barnabe, Giles. 'Chemin de Fer de la Baie de Somme: a postscript'. *Continental Modeller* June 1991 Vol. 13 No. 6 pp. 210-213.
Barnabe, Giles. 'French without tears: tips for modelling metre gauge stock'. *Continental Modeller* Vol. 19 No. 8 August 1997 pp. 343-347. Describes and illustrates several items of CFBS stock.
Burnham, Tom. 'Our twin in France'. *The Tenterden Terrier* [journal of the Kent & East Sussex Railway] No. 69 Spring 1996 pp. 17-21.
Cox, David and Pete Moragas. 'Chemin de Fer de la Baie de Somme'. *Continental Modeller* Nov./Dec. 1990 Vol. 12 No. 6 pp.234-239.
Davies, W.J.K. *French Minor Railways*. Dawlish: David & Charles; London: MacDonald, 1965.
Goodger, David. 'Excursion to Brighton'. *SNCF Society Journal* No. 90 June 1998 pp. 15-19.
Griffin, Trevor. 'Light railway survival'. *The Farmer's Line* [journal of the Kent & East Sussex Railway] Autumn 1970 pp. 57-59 and Summer 1971 pp. 81-83.
Haydock, David. 'Around the Somme Bay'. *Today's Railways* No. 7 June-July 1995 pp. 21-25.
Hitchcock, Paul. *The Narrow Gauge* No. 136 [n.d.] pp. 10-11.
Lommey, Peter. 'To the Somme with the L.C.G.B.' *The Narrow Gauge* No. 54 July 1970 pp. 31-32.
'Metre gauge on the Somme'. *Railway Magazine* May 1966 pp. 261-264.
Morgan, Bryan. *The End of the line*. London: Cleaver-Hulme Press, 1955.
Nickson, Geoffrey. 'Preservation on the Channel coast...French style!' *Narrow Gauge Times* Autumn 1978 pp. 10-14.

Pacey, Philip. 'Le Chemin de Fer de la Baie de Somme: Part 1 - from the beginnings to 1972'. *The Narrow Gauge* No. 141 [1994], pp. 14-20.
Pacey, Philip. 'Le Chemin de Fer de la Baie de Somme: Part 2 - The Preservation era'. *The Narrow Gauge* No. 142 [1994] pp. 8-14 .
Pacey, Philip. 'Le Chemin de Fer de la Baie de Somme: Part 3 - Addenda and Bibliography. *The Narrow Gauge* No. 145 [1995] pp. 26-29.
Pacey, Philip. 'A new lease of life for the Réseau des Bains de Mer'. *The Tenterden Terrier* No. 70 Summer 1996 pp. 36-41.
Rowe, D. Trevor (revised by W.J.K. Davies). 'C.F.E. Reseau de la Somme'. *The Railway Observer* Vol. XXXI No. 389 July 1961 pp. 210-211.
Rowe, D. Trevor. 'Steam around the Somme - a postscript'. *Narrow Gauge* No. 142 1994 p. 30. A note of a visit to the sugar beet refinery at Lanchères.
Sullivan, Tony. 'The Somme's charm offensive'. *Steam Classic* April/May 1998 pp. 56-57.

References

Chapter One
Béal, Jacques and Michel Desprez. *Au coeur de la Baie de Somme et du Marquenterre.* Tournai: La Renaissance du Livre, 1999. (A magnificent album of photographs by Michel Desprez.)
Béal, Jacques. 'Jules Verne en Somme'. *Revue Jules Verne* No. 4, 1997 pp. 55-60.
Cayeux d'hier. Abbeville: F. Paillart, [c.1985].
Cooper, Bill and Laurel. *Watersteps through France.* London: Methuen, 1991; Mandarin Paperbacks, 1992.
Le Crotoy d'hier. Abbeville: F. Paillart, [c. 1985].
Kendall, Richard. *Degas landscapes.* New Haven and London: Yale University Press, 1993.
Massart, Christian. *Cayeux.* Joue-les-Tours: Alan Sutton, 1996.
Le Nord: Picardie, Artois, Flandre, Ardenne. 4th ed. (Collection des Guides-Joanne). Paris: Librairie Hachette et Cie, 1914.
Noyon, Roger. 'Boudin à St Valery'. *Bulletin de la Société d'Archéologie et d'Histoire de Saint-Valery-sur-Somme du Ponthieu et du Vimeu* No.30 1999 pp. 4-7.
Saint-Valery d'hier. Abbeville: F. Paillart, 1985.
Taylor, Arthur R. *Spring on the Somme: a river journey.* London: Constable, 1995. Although there is no mention of the railways of the Baie de Somme, this account of a journey from the source of the Somme to St Valery is well worth reading for background information and pleasure.
Valicourt, Joseph de. *La Baie de Somme.* Noyelles: ISA Editions Sobanska, 1996.

Chapter Two
Arzul, Roland. 'La ligne à voie normale de Noyelles à St Valery'. *Ch'tchot Train* No. 26 Octobre 1995 p. 8-11; *Ch'tchot Train* 27 Décembre 1995 p. 4-5.
Banaudo, José. *Trains oubliés 4: Les Réseaux de l'Etat, du Nord et le Syndicat des Ceintures.* Breil-sur-Roya: Cabri, 1983.
Bulletin des Lois 1852 No. 496 p. 527. The 'Convention' of 19th February, 1852. This can also be found in:
    (1) *Annuaire-Chaix. Annuaire officiel des chemins de fer Année 1853.* Paris: Imprimerie et Librairie Centrales des Chemins de Fer de Napoléon Chaix et Cie, 1853 pp. 240- .
    (2) Chemin de Fer du Nord. *Documents officiels.* Lille: Imprimeries de L. Danel, 1857 pp. 107-111.
Bulletin des Lois 1854 No. 228 p. 624 . The 'Décret' of 17th October 1854. This can also be found in:
    (1) *Annuaire-Chaix. Annuaire officiel des chemins de fer Année 1855.* Paris: Imprimerie et Librairie Centrales des Chemins de Fer de Napoléon Chaix et Cie, 1855 pp. 493-495.
    (2) Chemin de Fer du Nord. *Documents officiels.* Lille: Imprimeries de L. Danel, 1857 pp. 122-125
Chemin de Fer du Nord. *Diagrammes et dimensions principales des locomotives du Réseau Français 1846-1884.* 1884.
Davies, John. *Chemins de Fer du Nord: locomotive list 1842-1938 with railcars.* Sunnybank, Queensland: John Davies, 1997.
Delattre, Jean. '1870 dans le canton de Saint-Valery'. *La Baie de Somme,* various issues, 1971. (This remarkable series of articles, which, incidentally, deals with the whole period of the Franco-Prussian War, including its aftermath, and not exclusively with the events of 1870, appeared in many successive issues of this weekly newspaper. The information I have used comes from the instalments published in No. 11, 20th March, and No. 12, 27th March).
Lambert, Henri. *Réseau du Nord: précis historique, statistique et financier.* Paris: H. Dunod et E. Pinat, 1909.
Lenne, Guy. 'L'Occasion manqué'. *Ch'tchot train* No. 41 Septembre 1999 p. 7-14.
Vilain, Lucien. *Dix decennies de locos sur le Réseau du Nord.* 1977.

Chapter Three
Arzul, Roland. 'Le réseau de la Somme des Chemins de Fer Economiques: Le groupe des bains de mer'. *Ch'tchot Train* No. 33 Juin 1997 pp. 6-8.
Banaudo, José. *Trains oubliés 4: Les Réseaux de l'Etat, du Nord et le Syndicat des Ceintures.* Breil-sur-Roya: Cabri, 1983.
Bulletin des Lois 1887 No. 1095 p. 1091 . The agreement between the Compagnie du Nord and the SE. This is also likely to have been printed in *Annuaire Chaix...1888,* and it can be found in: Chemin de Fer du Nord. *Documents officiels.* Lille: Imprimerie de L. Danel, 1894 pp. 285-294.
En ce temps là... la vapeur!... Les chemins de Fer du Nord. Paris: Rimage, 1979. Reprints extracts from a guide to seaside resorts served by the CF du Nord, published in 1911, and from the *Guide Baedeker* of 1893.
Goodger, David. 'Excursion to Brighton'. *The SNCF Society Journal* No. 90 June 1998 pp. 15-19.
Lomier, Eugène. *Le Chemin de fer de Noyelles à Saint-Valery sur Somme.* Amiens: Imprimerie des Echos Picards, 1936.
Pacey, Philip.'Les embranchements industriels sur le réseau: des bourgeons et des ramifications intéressants'. *Ch'tchot Train* No. 37 September 1998 pp.10-12.
Pérève, Guy. 'Le Réseau de la Somme des Chemins de Fer Economique'. *CFBS Bulletin* No. 3 Mars 1974 and No. 5 Juillet 1974, unnumbered pp.
Rapport présenté par le Conseil d'Administration de la Compagnie du chemin de fer du Nord à l'Assemblée Générale 1888.

Chapter Four
Arzul, Roland. 'La ligne des cent jours (1918)'. *Voie Etroite* 5/94 No. 144 Octobre/Novembre pp. 26-27.
Avril, Michel. *Raoul Dautry: la passion de servir.* Paris: France Empire, 1993.
Baudouï, Remi. *Raoul Dautry 1880-1951: le technocrate de la République.* Paris: Editions Balland, 1992.
Boissard de Senarpont, Raymond de. 'La ligne des 100 jours'. *Bulletin de la Société d'Archéologie et d'Histoire de Saint-Valery-sur-Somme, du Ponthieu et du Vimeu* No. 29 1998 pp. 30-37.
Davies, W.J.K. *Light railways of the First World War.* Newton Abbot: David & Charles, 1967.
Halperin, Vladimir. *Raoul Dautry: un batisseur de la SNCF au CEA.* Paris: Fayard, 1997.
Henniker, Col. A.M. *Transportation on the Western Front 1914-1918.* London: HMSO, 1937.
Lomier, Eugène. *Saint-Valery pendant la Grande Guerre 1914-1918.* St Valery: Imprimerie du Littoral de la Somme, 1922.
Pacey, Philip. 'La ligne des cent jours'. *SNCF Society Journal* No. 91 September 1998 pp. 34-35, 37.
Valicourt, Joseph de. *La Baie de Somme.* Noyelles: ISA Editions Sobanska, 1996.

Chapter Five
Garry, M.G. *La Baie de Somme et la Canal de la Somme: rapport de M.G.Garry,Président de la Chambre de Commerce d'Abbeville.* Abbeville: Imprimerie F. Paillart, 1920.
Lenne, Guy. 'Les automotrices'. *Ch'tchot Train* No. 39 Mars 1999 pp. 6-7, 10-11, 14-17.
Lenne, Guy. 'Les automotrices'. *Ch'tchot Train* No. 40 Julliet 1999 pp. 10-11, 14.
Lenne, Guy. 'Nos chers économiques'. *Ch'tchot Train* No. 37 Septembre 1998 pp. 14-15, 18.
Lomier, Eugène. *Le Chemin de Fer de Noyelles à Saint-Valery sur Somme.* Amiens: Imprimerie des Echos Picards, 1936.
Pérève, Guy. 'Le Réseau de la Somme des Chemins de Fer Economics'. *CFBS Bulletin* No. 3 Mars 1974 and No. 5 Juillet 1974, unnumbered pp.

Chapter Six
Arzul, Roland. 'La ligne de Lanchères à Ault'. *Ch'tchot Train* No. 25 Juillet 1995 pp. 6-9.
Béal, Jacques. *Hommes et combats en Picardie 1939/45.* 1994.
Béal, Jacques. *La Somme dans la guerre 1939/45.* 1986.
Chapuis, Jacques. 'Les voies ferrées ayant desservi Ault'. *Chemins de Fer Regionaux et Urbains* No. 249 1995/3 pp. 3-20.
Chazette, Alain (et al). *Atlantikwall: le Mur l'Atlantique en France 1940-1944.* Editions Heimdal, 1995.
Domengie, Henri et José Banaudo. *Les petits trains de jadis: Nord de la France.* 1995.
Estienne, Jean. 'La Fin des Bains de Mer'. *Pour le Littoral Picard et la Baie de Somme Bulletin* No. 11 Septembre 1997 pp. 12-22.
Lomier, Eugène. *Le Chemin de Fer de Noyelles à Saint-Valery sur Somme.* Amiens: Imprimerie des Echos Picards, 1936.
Pacey, Philip. 'Le Réseau des Bains de mer (Somme): la deuxième guerre mondiale: un chapitre oublié dans l'histoire du Réseau des Bains de Mer'. *Voie Etroite* 6/96 No. 157, Decembre/Janvier pp. 19-20.

Pacey, Philip. 'Le Réseau des Bains de Mer: l'horaire d'hiver Janvier 1944'. *Ch'tchot Train* No. 27 Décembre 1995 pp. 6-7.
Pacey, Philip. 'The 'Réseau des Bains de Mer' in the Second World War'. *World War Two Railway Study Group Bulletin* Vol. 8 No. 1 January/February 1998 p. 21-25.
Partridge, Colin. *Hitler's Atlantic Wall*. Guernsey: DI Publications 1976.
Salmon, Robert. *Autrefois le tortillard de Woincourt à Ault (Onival): complément*. Abbeville: Edition Les Vedettes Picardes, n.d.
Séries Bleue 1:25000, No. 2007. 1988. [This marvellous large scale map marks surviving German blockhouses].
Additional information was also obtained from:
Valicourt, Joseph de. *La Baie de Somme*. Noyelles: ISA Editions Sobanska, 1996.
Marie-Christine Mopin [information concerning Cayeux during the War].
Air Photograph Library, University of Keele.
K.W. Clingan [information regarding the locomotives left by the Germans at St Valery].
L'Ecomusée, Le Creusot [information regarding the Schneider 0-6-2T locomotive at St Valery].

Chapter Seven
Allen, Peter and P.B.Whitehouse. *Narrow Gauge Railways of Europe*. London: Ian Allan, 1959.
Davies, W.J.K. *French Minor Railways*.
Girode, C.E. 'Lanchères juillet 1965'. *Ch'tchot Train* No. 27.
Griffin, Trevor. 'Light railway survival'. *The Farmer's Line*, Autumn 1970 p. 57-59; Summer 1971 p. 81-83.
'Le Groupe des 'Bains de Mer' de Réseau de la Somme'. *La Vie du Rail* No. 663 1958 pp. 16-21.
Lemmey, Peter. 'To the Somme with the L.C.G.B.'. *The Narrow Gauge* No. 54 July 1970.
'Metre gauge on the Somme'. *Railway Magazine* May 1966 p. 261-264.
'La Mise à voie normale des lignes du Crotoy et de Saint-Valery'. *Ch'tchot Train* No. 31 Dècembre 1996 p. 10-11.
Morgan, Bryan. *The End of the line*. London: Cleaver-Hulme Press, 1955.
Paul, Petit. *Le Temps de l'apprentissage: souvenirs de jeunesse 1940-1945*. Arras: Littéra, 1993. (This is the source of my information about the strike in May 1945. Unfortunately neither the reason for nor the length of the strike are stated, and at the time of going to press no further information was to hand.)
Rowe, D. Trevor (with revision by W.J.K. Davies). 'C.F.E. Reseau de la Somme'. *The Railway Observer* Vol. XXXI No. 389 July 1961 p. 210-211.

Chapter Eight
'Convention de mise à disposition de biens et d'ouvrages d'interêts ferroviaires'. *Ch'tchot Train* no. 36 Juin 1998 pp. 6-7. The text of the agreement with the Département signed on 25th April, 1998.
Girode, C.E. 'Trente ans!' *Ch'tchot Train* No. 40 Juillet 1999 p.15.
Testu, Maurice. 'Histoire du CFBS'. *Ch'tchot Train* no. 21 Mars 1994 pp.14-15, No. 22 Octobre 1994 p. 6-7, No. 23 Décembre 1994 pp. 10-11, No. 29 Juin 1996 p.14, No. 31 Décembre 1996 pp. 6-7, No. 35 Décembre 1997 p.6.
Testu, Maurice, 'L'Histoire du Chemin de Fer da la Baie de Somme', *Chemins de Fer Régionaux & Urbains* No. 273, 3/1999 pp. 4-26.
The Tenterden Terrier No. 70 Summer 1996 includes descriptions and photographs of the twinning ceremony and steam festival in April 1996, as does *Ch'tchot Train* no. 29 Juin, 1996.

Appendix One
Etat génèrale des locomotives (document 1996027 0367 in the Archives at Roubaix). An SE document comprising a detailed list of locomotives in service in 1922/23(?).
Lenne, Guy. 'Les automotrices'. *Ch'tchot Train* No. 39 Mars 1999 pp. 6-7, 10-11, 14-17.
Lenne, Guy. 'Les automotrices'. *Ch'tchot Train* No. 40 Julliet 1999 pp. 10-11, 14.
Pérève, Guy. 'Le Réseau de la Somme des Chemins de Fer Economique'. *CFBS Bulletin* No. 3 Mars 1974 and No. 5 Juillet 1974, unnumbered pp.
Additional information was also received from Keith Clingan and Guy Laplanche.